THE
TIME
TEAM
DIG BOOK

THE
TIME
TEAM
DIG BOOK

TIM TAYLOR

Books

CONTENTS

INTRODUCTION

WELCOME TO THE *Time Team Dig Book*. The year 2012 was a momentous one for the series: we crossed the 225 total for the number of programmes made to date, and we also saw the end of this particular stage of *Time Team*'s story. In this book I hope to give you an idea of some of the key skills we have used over more than twenty years of excavation, setting those skills in the context of the archaeological digs we completed during the past year.

So where did this all begin? *Time Team* was a format I created in 1992, based on a series of documentaries called *Time Signs*, which followed archaeological work in the Roadford Valley, near Exeter, as sites were excavated prior to the valley being flooded to create a new reservoir. Devon county archaeologist Simon Timms gave us a lot of support and recommended Mick Aston when I needed an archaeologist to tell the story of the valley. Mick suggested Phil Harding as a good person to undertake the reconstructions of prehistoric skills. And the rest is history!

BELOW: *Neil Holbrook leads a discussion on tactics. Where should that first trench go in?*

ABOVE: *Soil flies through the air as Phil gets stuck into a trench.*

The way *Time Team* works has been for over twenty years a challenge for the wider world of archaeology. To achieve what we set out to do in three days is remarkable, and archaeologists have been right to question the basic model. If *Time Team* can show that it is possible to analyse sites in three days based on small-scale evaluations of geophysics surveys, this has a fundamental implication for how we evaluate sites in the future, although of course not all sites are suited to this approach. There are three obvious elements that make the *Time Team* approach feasible. We limit ourselves to answering specific questions; we bring in every available resource to support the process; and we select sites that have good potential for evaluation via geophysics. From the start we have been led by geophysics; *Time Team* is much more of a geophysics evaluation process than is sometimes obvious.

Time Team began as a model with limited ambitions. The sites were often in people's back gardens; we rarely took on larger, nationally important sites. This soon changed as archaeologists began to realize what could be achieved by working with us. Over the last ten years, we have increasingly been offered larger, more important sites by archaeologists at English Heritage and CADW and by county archaeologists. Our list of digs includes Westminster Abbey, the Queen's Royal Palaces, Hadrian's Wall and one of the country's biggest Saxon hall sites at Sutton Courtenay, and more than fifty Scheduled Ancient Monuments.

We developed a unique model, which, put at its simplest, aimed to evaluate key questions on major sites in three days. This work was entirely self-funded, with the production budget funding recording, report-writing and post-excavation analysis and care of finds. There are now more than 220 sites that have been excavated and funded by *Time Team*, with approximately 98 per cent of those having been written up in reports. Over the last ten years the recording process has been the responsibility of Wessex Archaeology, one of the largest commercial archaeological practices in the UK. The series has been broadcast in more than thirty-six countries worldwide and has received numerous awards, including two Royal Television Society awards and a nomination for a Bafta.

It has been estimated that over the last twenty years *Time Team* has put over £4 million into research archaeology, making us one of the major funders of archaeology in the UK. This funding was of course dependent on the programme being sufficiently popular with the general public for a broadcaster to commission further series. The model we have followed had the unique

OPPOSITE: *Rob Hedge and Raksha Dave reveal a wall. Note the ever-present polythene sheet laid down to stop the soil damaging the turf.*

LEFT: *Stewart shows Tony the results of his topographic survey.*

capacity to combine three elements: the archaeological instincts of our team, the geophysical skills of GSB, and a creative filming response that captured the process in a way that appealed to television audiences. We were lucky to have a fine creative team, led by directors like Graham Dixon and cameramen like Nick Dance and Clive North, who were capable of following the unpredictable process of archaeologists making discoveries on the hoof.

Behind it all was a team of individuals who I regarded as the *Time Team* family. Between them they provided the expertise we needed on each site at the highest level. Whenever a specific skill was required, we were pretty much able to find the best person in the country to join us. Over the years these individuals became a band of regulars whose faces will be familiar to anyone who watches the show.

I have often wondered what a *Time Team* university course on archaeology might look like

if we could bring all these people together in one place. If we were asked by the Open University or a similar organization to create a syllabus, what would be in it? We have often sat down during a shoot and made a list of the obvious key skills, but we quickly realized that a set of abstract skills described independently from the digs would end up being rather dry. It would fail to capture the essential element of the *Time Team* programmes: the application of archaeology to the reality of specific sites. Learning a set of skills away from the usual array of difficulties that we face in every programme would mean that the critical aspect of carrying out archaeology in the field was lost.

I felt that the best introduction to the subject would be to allow readers to follow us on a dig each day and see how we adapt archaeological skills to the challenges of each location. If you want to learn how to interpret the lumps and bumps of a landscape, I can think of no better way to find out than to follow Stewart Ainsworth for

RIGHT: *Filming Phil during the making of the* Time Signs *documentary series in 1992. Holding the monitor is Martin Lee, who would go on to become one of* Time Team's *top editors.*

the duration of a programme. Sitting by a trench as Phil Harding explains the subtleties of stratigraphy is equally enlightening, as is following John Gater as he uses geophysics to interpret what may be beneath the ground.

What follows is an attempt to get as near as we can to that process in a book. We will be taking you through a year of *Time Team* digs, and along the way we will show you how we have applied most of the key archaeological skills and used them to solve the specific problems of individual sites. We have provided examples of pottery types from each period, as the identification of pottery is so important to dating a site. You will also be able to see the computer reconstructions and the illustrations by Victor Ambrus of how sites would have looked in the past. After more than 200 programmes, we've learned that one of the things viewers most like to see is Victor's drawings, which bring the past to life so vividly.

We've included Tony's opening pieces to camera – which usually end with the words 'and we've only got three days' – so that you can see how our expectations at the start have to be

adjusted as we encounter the realities in the trenches. We have also outlined the key archaeological goals set out in the project design that we create for each programme, in cooperation with local archaeologists, English Heritage inspectors and other interested parties.

On every *Time Team* shoot, we not only have a group of the country's best archaeologists at hand, but also a wide range of experts on relevant subjects that help us to evaluate each site. It's by bringing together the best possible team that we are able to take on a site in such a short timescale. It has always been my job to push the team along – probably a bit faster than they would go otherwise – and make sure the television side is not making up a reality it would like to believe, rather than the one that is actually there in the trenches.

This book will give you access to the collective wisdom of the *Time Team* academy of experts, and I hope it will give you an idea of how they work as they face the real challenge of excavation against the clock. It should also answer some of the typical questions we are asked. How do we set up a site, obtain permissions, negotiate with landowners and English Heritage, and so on? What happens after we have finished a dig: how do the backfill team operate and who records the trench? What happens to the finds? How do we clean finds on site and how do we date the stratigraphy in a trench? And what exactly is in Phil's box?

I have always thought that if I wanted to know how to go about the different aspects of archaeology, I could think of no better guides than the experts who've worked on *Time Team* for over twenty years. This book will, I hope, give you access to some of the secrets behind their skills. It may also encourage you to revisit some of our previous digs, which are available to watch via Channel 4's 4 on Demand service.

All of the 200-plus *Time Team* excavations have taken place without any support from public funds. The excavation surveys and reports available on the Wessex Archaeology website have been funded by the programme. *Time Team* is the second-largest funder of archaeology in the UK after English Heritage, and the archive of sites we have excavated represents a unique legacy that will go on assisting British archaeologists in the future.

I hope you enjoy the team's introduction to some of the basic archaeological skills and how they are applied in practice. We want to inspire readers to learn more about this fascinating subject and hopefully get out and undertake some archaeology themselves. To find out more, you can join the *Time Team* club at: www. timeteamdigital.com.

BELOW: *Taking time to have a chat with Tony at Brancaster.*

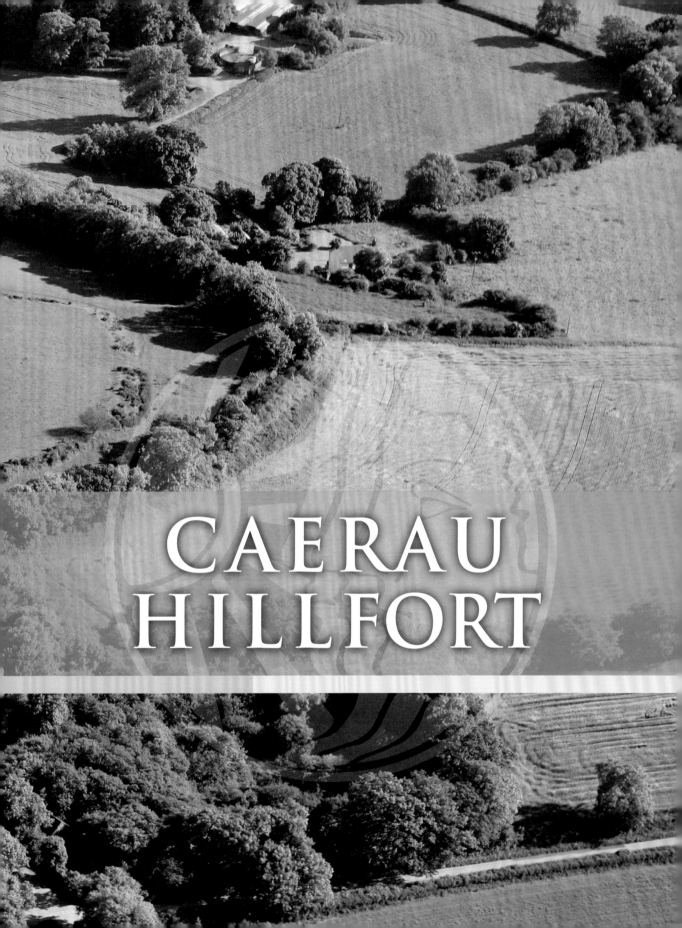

CAERAU
HILLFORT

This is an example of a site where a huge archaeological monument exists within a large community on the edge of Cardiff, the largest city in Wales, and yet is relatively unknown to the people who live there.

OF THE MILLIONS of people who drive along the M4 and the M50 to Cardiff and have to divert around a huge hill, few will realize that on the crest of the hill there was once a vast Iron Age hillfort – possibly one of the biggest in Wales. We were lucky to be working at this site with Niall Sharples, who is an expert on the Iron Age in Wales and was able to guide us during the initial stages of our work towards the right targets.

Iron Age hillforts are quite a big site to bite off in just three days, and targeting our work was going to be critical. At an early stage we had the advantage of a LiDAR survey (see Mini Skills Masterclass, page 19) which enabled us to get an idea of the topography of the site. What is particularly useful about this kind of survey is that it removes the tree canopy and allows you to see the huge ditches that were dug to protect the fort. One of the key questions about these sites is centred on the argument between those who regard them as having a fundamentally military and strategic role, and those who regard them as a monument whose main function was to impress neighbours and help to establish the power of an Iron Age chief.

Some of the key elements were already in place: we had Paul Blinkhorn to advise us on pottery, and with Francis Pryor on board we were not going to be short of expertise on the prehistoric age. Early on the morning of Day One, before Tony's opening piece to camera, I took advantage of the peace and quiet and went for a walk along the ditches and banks with Niall. These are incredibly impressive and always make me wonder about the social organization that would have been needed to get this kind of work done. Were there slaves involved in moving the thousands of tons of soil required to create the defensive ditches, or was this achieved by local communities coming together, united by their desire to create an impressive monument?

Niall had some very interesting things to say about the strategic and military aspect of Iron Age life. As we climbed along the ditches and

scrambled over branches and slid down the steep sides of the fortifications, he made the point that military defence and aggression in the Iron Age may well have been based on a model nearer to guerrilla warfare than one built around huge, strategically located forts. With a potential attacker like the Romans or a rival tribe, concentrating all your assets in a single location may well have been counterproductive, as it made it only too obvious which points in the landscape needed to be attacked. When one thinks of the Roman arsenal of weapons available to attack static sites, this lends weight to Niall's view that small dispersed bands carrying out guerrilla warfare would have been the most successful response.

Jim Mower, the Development Producer, had worked with both CADW and Dr Oliver Davis at Cardiff University to develop the project design, and this set out the research aims for our work, which were as follows:

ABOVE LEFT: *Aerial view of the Caerau site. The later church and earthworks can be seen on the right.*

LEFT: *Niall Sharples, our key archaeologist, on the first morning at Caerau. The Land Rover created a useful windbreak on a freezing cold morning.*

HOW TO IDENTIFY IRON AGE HILLFORTS

Scattered across the British landscape are an impressive type of earthwork known as a hillfort. Although various sites of defended hilltops have been attributed to the Neolithic period and the Bronze Age, the great period of fort construction was during the Iron Age, between 700 BC and the Roman invasion in AD 43. A vast spectrum of shapes and sizes of fort exist, from small homesteads of under an acre to enclosures of over 200 acres. Two common types of hillfort were the contour fort, which has a bank and ditch dug along the contour line enclosing an area of high ground, and the promontory fort, positioned on a spur of land with a bank and ditch dug across the neck of the promontory and making use of the pre-existing natural defences for the other sides. Perhaps the most famous and largest Iron Age hillfort in Europe is Maiden Castle in Dorset. Excavated by the influential archaeologist Sir Mortimer Wheeler from 1934 to 1938, the site is a vast enclosure covering an area the size of fifty football pitches.

Today all that remains on hillfort sites are banks and ditches known as ramparts. A univallate hillfort consists of an area enclosed by a single bank and ditch; a bivallate has two lines of defence; while multivallate hillforts have three or more ditches. Ramparts were made from timber, stone or earth, depending on what material was most readily available. Archaeological evidence has also shown that on some sites the bank was topped with a palisade, vastly improving defence.

The debate around the function of hillforts continues. Until recently, they were presumed to be associated with combat and defence, as their

ABOVE: *Aerial view of Maiden Castle, the classic Iron Age hillfort site in Dorset.*

name reflects; the term hillfort was first used in 1931. Over the past two decades, archaeological investigation has uncovered evidence of settlement and ritual practices occurring within hillforts, and indications that the structures were also used for storage of grain and weaponry. This has sparked theories circulating around the idea that these earthworks were public monuments associated with agricultural cycles and grain production, or a type of communal centre for the local population, where the drama of ceremony and ritual could take place. The question of the hillfort's main purpose remains unresolved.

Other notable Iron Age hillforts in Wales include Caer y Twr Hillfort in Anglesey, Tre'r Ceiri Hillfort in Gwynedd and Castell Henllys Hillfort in Pembroke.

TONY'S PIECE TO CAMERA

❝ *I'm standing on the edge of what may be an ancient tribal capital in a most unlikely place: Ely housing estate, in the heart of South Wales.*

This giant hill is the mysterious Caerau. No one has dug here before. But it may have been a vital stronghold for Welsh tribes that lived here over two thousand years ago.

Could this be the long lost capital of South Wales? Although the thing about long lost places is you never know what you're going to find there … **❞**

Research aim 1: What is the extent and layout of surviving archaeological remains and of any settlement within the defended closure at Caerau Hillfort?

Research aim 2: What is the character and chronology of any surviving internal structures at Caerau Hillfort?

Research aim 3: Assuming the multivallate defended enclosure (hillfort) at Caerau is Iron Age, is there surviving evidence of an earlier hillfort at the site?

Research aim 4: To answer the question: was there Roman occupation of the site, possibly in the first century AD?

Close to Caerau is the Roman villa at Ely, which was excavated in 1894 and then again in 1922 by Sir Mortimer Wheeler, and small amounts of Roman pottery had turned up on the site, including a piece of a mortarium. It is interesting that on a site like this, Roman activity is discussed in terms of an 'invasion period' – a reminder that not all British Iron Age tribes welcomed the Romans with open arms. Archaeologists in the past tended to emphasize that British tribes were developing trading relationships with the Romans prior to the invasion. This was certainly not the case throughout the country; even in eastern Britain the Romans often had to apply their military might to subdue the local tribes, particularly after the Boudiccan revolt.

As usual on *Time Team*, the first step was to get the geophysics team in and a decision was made to analyse a small strip in the middle of the site. However, Francis was keen to look at a ditch that appeared to divide off one side of the site from the other; these kinds of sites are often divided in this way. This can be a strategic division, providing additional defence or related to dividing livestock from living areas.

Matt began work on the ditch area. This gave us a chance to discuss further with Niall the likely origins of the site: as he put it, 'these sites defined and created an identity for the people who lived here'. Towards the end of the Bronze Age, people were living in small isolated farmsteads and then around 800 BC there was a huge transition where people began to collect together on these kinds of sites. According to Niall, the purpose of this may not necessarily have been military; however, the ramparts, which are huge, would have clearly provided a considerable obstacle to anybody thinking of attacking the site.

ABOVE: *John showing us the first set of geophysics results. They weren't quite as clear as we had hoped!*

BELOW: *Victor's drawing of an Iron Age roundhouse, typical of the structures that would have been found at Caerau.*

Tony pointed out that Niall's view seemed to ignore the military potential: as he remarked, 'You make it sound like something built by the social services.' Whatever the purpose of the structure, we were clearly dealing with a vast monument, one of the biggest hillforts in South Wales and something that may have been the equivalent of the capital city for the tribe that occupied it. According to Tacitus, who gives a very detailed description of the Iron Age tribes of Wales, this area was occupied by the Silures, who were famous for their ferocious defence of their homeland and who waged a thirty-year guerrilla battle against the Roman invaders. There is a reference by Roman historians to a captured leader of the Silures, who was taken to Rome and made a speech in front of his captors that was so moving and powerful that

HOW DOES LiDAR WORK?

Light Detection and Ranging (LiDAR) is a relatively new surveying technique that operates using a pulsed laser beam attached to an aircraft. The laser beam scans from side to side, recording between 20,000 to 100,000 pulses per second as the aircraft flies over the survey area. For every individual laser pulse, some of the energy is reflected back to the equipment on board the aircraft. The time it takes for the reflection to reach the equipment is measured, and this data is then used to build a detailed high-resolution three-dimensional model of the ground. This allows archaeologists to 'fly' around the landscape on a computer screen, looking for features of possible archaeological interest and examining them from different angles. Flying makes it possible to survey a large area, meaning many of the archaeological features can be seen within the wider landscape.

Unlike other methods of aerial survey, such as aerial photography, LiDAR can penetrate vegetation and map the topography underneath –

an invaluable feature at the Caerau site. When the aircraft flies over woodland, laser-pulse energy is reflected back from the upper tree canopy, the lower tree canopy, the ground vegetation and the true ground surface. This allows for a whole series of layers to be produced for every single laser pulse. The system works best during the winter months when there is less vegetation and the laser energy can pass directly to the ground, giving the clearest results. Computer processing filters the results, allowing for the ground surface to be modelled at a very high resolution in three dimensions and potentially revealing archaeological earthworks that may never previously have been seen in aerial photographs. The technique is particularly suited to linear features; it has previously shown very subtle earthworks that would have been difficult to spot on the ground.

Despite its advantages, LiDAR has some limitations that prevent it from being the answer to every archaeologist's prayers. Firstly, many flight and laser configuration variables can affect the final resolution of the survey, and even if surveying takes place in the winter, not all canopy and ground vegetation types are equally porous to the laser energy, which can skew the data. It is also inevitable that the system may not show very discrete small features: although computer processing to remove vegetation cover can be helpful, it can also either hide or remove these subtle features. Finally, LiDAR also cannot differentiate between modern, archaeological or vegetation-produced features. Therefore, while LiDAR can be very helpful in spotting potential archaeological features, the best technique for investigating further remains the traditional one – heading out into the field and having a good look.

ABOVE: *Emma's LiDAR image and the geophysics survey set within it. You may just be able to make out small circular features, which indicate roundhouses.*

RIGHT: *Adding copper ore to the furnace to create the handle for our bronze drinking vessel.*

he and his family were set free. It would be interesting to know whether that speech was made in Welsh.

If this site was as important as it appeared, we would surely find evidence of many people having lived here. Caerau is a natural hill that must have always appealed to local inhabitants as a site that could be easily defended. It is likely that the first Iron Age occupation began around 650 BC and lasted until the appearance of the Romans some time after AD 43. At this time there would have been local Welsh people occupying the site, but possibly trading with Romans and adopting some aspects of Roman life.

In the first trench put across Francis's ditch Matt began to uncover large areas of grey silt. Ditches are very useful on sites like this because they tend to accumulate bits of pottery from those living on the site, often preserved by the damp clay and mud which can be found at the base.

By 10.30 a.m. we were beginning to get our first geophysics results, which were frankly rather disappointing. However, there was just enough of a hint of a curved ditch for Phil to place a trench to investigate whether this was our first roundhouse. As he pointed out, roundhouses are made of mud, thatch and a small amount of stone. They easily dissolve over time into the surrounding landscape, and finding them has always been a matter of looking for stains and small insignificant features in the ground.

Francis had directed the geophysics team to make the next scan alongside the inside of the rampart. Roundhouses in this area may well have been better protected due to the accumulation of soil against the face of the rampart. Around noon on Day One this approach came up trumps, and we were at last able to see the faint signs of several roundhouses. This would be the site of our third trench. Francis's plan was to dig a trench from what was effectively the front door to the middle of the feature.

At the start of Day Two the geophysics team had been able to work on their results, and Niall and Francis now felt they were able to see at least ten possible roundhouses.

THIS SUGGESTED THE population could have been over 100 in what amounted to about 10 per cent of the site. The problem facing us was to find dating evidence that would confirm that these features were Iron Age and allow us to suggest that they had existed at the same time. Sites like this are occupied over a number of years, and there is evidence in Wales for Iron Age occupation on hillforts lasting from 800 BC to AD 100 – exactly the period our houses belonged to.

From the start of Trench 3 we began to face some difficulties. Francis was convinced that one of the features we were looking at was glacial. John disagreed, still believing his geophysics showed the curve of a roundhouse wall. In order for this question to be resolved, the trench had to be made much bigger.

Back in Trench 1, Matt and Raksha had enlisted the help of some of the local residents, giving them a chance to experience scraping away at the archaeology. Our visitors included children from the local estate who were part of an organization called Care Heritage, formed to help and develop an interest in local history. Francis's ditch was clearly quite shallow and not yet at a level that would give us any Iron Age artefacts.

RIGHT: *Phil working in Trench 1. Note the metal rods with orange caps: these are used to mark fixed points within the excavation.*

ABOVE: *Pottery expert Paul Blinkhorn and a group of children from the local community get a chance to look around the site.*

ABOVE: *Cassie with the finished drinking vessel, restraining herself from taking a long drink after a hard day's work!*

BELOW: *Cassie waiting to break the mould and reveal the bronze handle for the drinking vessel.*

With work proceeding in the trenches, we were able to take a look at some of the beautiful finds in the National Museum of Wales that came from this area in the Iron Age. The artefacts included bronze bracelets and decorative mounts from horses and chariots, illustrating the skill and artistic ability of our Iron Age ancestors. Danni Wootton, our small finds expert, was particularly taken with an Iron Age drinking vessel, and we decided to see if we could reconstruct one of these in order to create our own community drinking cup over the next couple of days.

In one corner of the field we set up our own bronze metallurgy centre, with experts turning

LEFT: *Francis shows Tony one of our first significant finds: an Iron Age quern stone.*

copper ore into bronze (see mini skills masterclass on page 25). As Niall explained, bronze was still an important material during the Iron Age and was particularly used to make small bronze handles decorated with Iron Age motifs.

Around 10.30 a.m. on Day Two we encountered our first significant find: a quern stone, used for turning wheat into flour. We have found a number of these on Iron Age sites. In some cases they seem to act as a closing deposit, marking the end of a period of occupation. The exciting thing from Francis's point of view was that this meant we had evidence of people grinding wheat on this site.

After lunch on Day Two it was decided to put a fourth trench over the oval enclosure that could be seen on the geophysics results. The enclosure had a distinctive entrance break, which may have been the entrance for the whole site. At this point in the Iron Age, there are often deposits made in the terminal end of the ditch; it was decided to site our trench over one of the features.

Close-up of the quern stone, showing the central groove.

ABOVE: *Ian Powlesland excavating the terminal end of a ditch, which turned out to be later than Iron Age.*

It was now nearly halfway through our shoot and yet we still had very little evidence of Iron Age or other artefacts. Phil appeared to have some post holes in his trench, which can be a good source of finds, but as we approached the end of Day Two solid evidence was proving elusive. The day ended with the magical appearance of molten bronze, which would be used to create the handles for our drinking cup. As Tony tapped the mould away, he reflected that this was probably the first time bronze had been created on this site for over two thousand years.

WHAT IS EXPERIMENTAL ARCHAEOLOGY?

Experimental archaeology, sometimes known as reconstruction archaeology, involves the recreation of ancient structures and artefacts using what are believed to be historically accurate technologies. Experimental archaeology is used to provide evidence for a variety of problems, from complete working replicas of Iron Age farmsteads, which allow for long-term experiments into prehistoric agriculture, to the construction of modern earthworks in order to measure the effects of weathering on ditches and banks, enabling archaeologists to better understand how ancient monuments would have looked. In addition to these large-scale monuments and ancient structures, smaller individual artefacts are often created, such as the Iron Age drinking vessel at the Caerau site. Experimental archaeologists will equip modern professional butchers, archers and lumberjacks with replica tools, based on ones recovered from the archaeological record, in order to see how effective they would have been for certain tasks. This hands-on approach allows for many interesting insights into both the artefacts and the technologies used to make them.

How is bronze made?

In order to make our Iron Age drinking vessel at Caerau, a bronze forge was set up. To successfully create bronze we needed a furnace capable of reaching over 1,000 degrees Centigrade, as bronze is created by melting down copper and mixing it with a small amount of tin. Although the quantities vary, a good general ratio is roughly 90 per cent copper and 10 per cent tin. Pure copper is too soft to make decent tools, while tin on its own is too brittle

and breaks easily. However, an alloy of the two materials becomes much harder and less brittle, making a better material for tools and statues.

Various copper deposits existed and were put to use by the inhabitants of hillforts such as Caerau across Wales and England. Perhaps the most important of these yet discovered is the Great Orme Mines in Llandudno, where there are copper extractions dating back to the Bronze Age. It has been estimated that 1,800 tonnes of copper ore were lifted out of the ground at Great Orme by prehistoric Britons. During the Iron Age, Europe had very few sources of tin. Fortunately for the inhabitants of Caerau, Devon and Cornwall were one of the few areas where tin was readily available on the ground surface, providing a nearby source. When these above-ground deposits were exhausted, the inhabitants of Devon and Cornwall turned to mining, which continued in the area until the twentieth century.

ABOVE: *A crucible of copper ore waiting to go into the furnace.*

At the start of Day Three we were able to see, as the LiDAR results process had emphasized, what an impressive site this was.

THE RESULTS CLEARLY showed that our trench had terminal ends and the enclosure was not far away from the entrance. Ian Powesland's excavation in this area had begun to produce pottery, but the majority of it was turning out to be Roman! Was it possible that some of the factors we were looking at related to a Roman farmstead?

With just one day left, Francis revisited the geophysics. If we could locate where hearths had existed inside roundhouses, this would help us to find more structures on the site. Where the geophysics showed a strong circular feature with a significant hot spot on the magnetometry indicating a fire or hearth, this implied the location of at least one family unit. Trench 5 went in on one of these anomalies.

With time rapidly running out, Naomi and Tracey at last began to find some fragments of Iron Age pottery in Trench 3, our first roundhouse ditch. Importantly, these fragments of pottery were well stratified in post holes. Paul Blinkhorn was able to identify these finds as Iron Age, probably coming from a small drinking cup and a large storage vessel that might have held the mead or beer for the family. Naomi's careful excavation meant that she was able to lift two pieces of the drinking vessel from the trench, which looked like they could be reconstructed, having a complete profile from rim to base.

RIGHT: *Niall Sharples and Paul Blinkhorn getting excited about the piece of Iron Age pot we found.*

A close-up shows the curved surface and base of the Iron Age cup.

ABOVE: *Paul carefully cleaning what would turn out to be our key find. A pottery sherd of this size from the Iron Age is fairly rare.*

HOW TO IDENTIFY POTTERY

When it comes to identifying pottery, the most helpful pieces are known as 'feature sherds'. These are the fragments from an area of the pot including a rim, a base or some decoration. Finding a feature sherd can make the job of identification a lot easier. Unfortunately, most of the time archaeologists are identifying plain body sherds, which bear fewer tell-tale indicators. When trying to identify a piece of ancient pottery, the three key factors to take into consideration are: the pot's fabric and inclusions – what it's made of and any other bits of material within the clay; the way the pot was made, which can affect its form or shape; and finally the finish or decoration applied to it.

First, the fabric or inclusions: these change according to both the geology and developments in ceramic technology. The geology in this country is very mixed: for instance, if you are in Northamptonshire the clay tends to contain a lot of shelly limestone, whereas in Leicestershire the clay contains a lot more granite. While inclusions such as fine sand do occur naturally within clay, it is sometimes the case that particular inclusions are added deliberately as

ABOVE: *Grass-tempered Anglo-Saxon pottery found at a site in west London.*

ABOVE: *A piece of pottery found at Caerau, probably Iron Age. Note the layered effect of poorly fired pottery.*

people experiment with clay. An example of this can be seen in early Saxon pottery, where large chunks of crushed rock were added by the potter in order to make the clay stiffer, easier to work and less likely to crack under heating.

The next stage of pottery identification is determining how a piece of pottery was made. There are three basic ways of making pottery. The first, hand building, is where you start with a lump of clay which you either pinch into a pot shape or roll into coils and build up before smoothing the edges down. The two other methods are based around wheel-throwing methods. One is known as a 'slow wheel', which isn't really a wheel but more of a turntable, similar in design to the platform you would ice a cake on. In this method, the pot is built up by adding coil upon coil on the turntable, smoothing and turning as you go. When the construction is complete, the wheel is spun, and the weight of the finished pot acts as a fly wheel, making it possible to smooth and even the pot's sides. The final method is the continually rotating potter's wheel, still popular among craft groups and small potters today. Using this method, it is possible to

ABOVE: *A selection of pottery from the* Time Team *dig at Burslem.*

throw a nice big, thin-walled pot. The best way to tell how your bit of pottery was made is to look closely at the individual marks left by the potter's hands. Pots that have been hand-built will often display finger marks, while pots thrown on a wheel are more likely to be uniform and smooth. Unfortunately, these methods are unlikely to reveal the date a pot was made, as the individual methods have gone in and out of favour across long periods of time.

The third and final factor that helps in the identification of pottery is the finish or decoration. There are a huge variety of finishes, including slips, glazes and burnishes, that can help distinguish the dates and geography of pots. Slips are a common form of decoration in which the pot is coated with a wash (the slip) of thin clay of a contrasting colour. Slipped pottery first became common in the Roman period, the most famous type being the glossy red or orange samian ware. Glazes are also common, particularly on modern pottery; they are rarely found on pottery from Roman Britain and never on prehistoric items. Aside from decoration, glazes act as a way of making pottery watertight. Adding a glaze to a pot can be achieved in a number of ways, from applying dry powdered material to covering it with a solution of chemicals in water. A huge variety of glazes exist; three common ones that often crop up on archaeological sites are clear glaze, tin glaze and salt glazes. Burnishes are created using a stone or another tool to smooth the surface of an unfired pot, reducing its porosity. During the Romano-British period, burnishing was used to create a smooth sheen over the entire pot.

As with finishes, a huge array of decoration types exist and these can help us in narrowing down a particular type of pot. The type of decoration is often linked to technological skills, but this is not a definite dating technique – examples of all decoration styles are still widely in use today. The simpler forms of decoration include impressing, stamping, rouletting, incising and combing, all of which involve using tools and objects to mark patterns onto the clay. More complicated techniques such as applied decoration and relief modelling were developed, but this was not until the late Roman period.

Paul Blinkhorn

ABOVE: *Black burnished ware found at Brancaster.*

IRON AGE POTTERY

Identifying Iron Age pottery

The best way to identify Iron Age pottery is to use the principles explained on the previous page. The first thing to note is that inclusions vary throughout the period. Pottery from the early Iron Age contains a lot of flint inclusions; by the middle Iron Age more shell can be seen; while pots from the later Iron Age tend to contain 'grog' – crushed pieces of fired clay. The potter's wheel was introduced to Britain during the Iron Age, so some pots were still being made using the coil method, while others were constructed on the wheel. The shape of pots tended to change over time. During the early Iron Age, pots tended to have fairly sharp, well-defined shoulders; while in the middle and late Iron Age, these shoulders tended to become less well defined and a bit 'slacker'. If you have a big enough piece to examine, the shape can be a useful dating indication, although this is certainly not an exact science. Lastly, the decoration is a very useful identification tool.

The early Iron Age exhibits decoration such as fingertip marks on the shoulders of the pots; while during the middle of the Iron Age, deep scouring across the body of the pot can often be seen. Interestingly, towards the end of the Iron Age it appears that many pots and vessels were largely undecorated, apart from certain areas which exhibit beautiful examples of La Tène decoration.

Although these approaches to identification are a good place to start, it is important to remember that they are very generalized. Inclusion, shape and decoration varied around the country: pottery has always been very regional and this was particularly so in the Iron Age. Unlike other periods, such as the Roman era, where there were a lot of large industrial sites with kilns churning out vast quantities of pottery, during the Iron Age manufacture appears to have been much more localized. Although we don't know for sure, it is generally assumed people were more or less making their own pottery, so if you needed a pot, you simply went and dug up the clay and made one, rather than buying one from your local potter.

Therefore, if you are interested in identifying a piece of pottery, the best way to start is by researching Iron Age pottery in the local area, or seeking advice from a local expert.

Paul Blinkhorn

LEFT: *A close-up of some Iron Age pottery. Note the obvious inclusions.*

ABOVE: *Finds expert Danni Wootton manages to get hold of the drinking vessel and try the local ale.*

When Niall saw this pottery he was ecstatic: he described it as the most complete Iron Age drinking cup ever found in South Wales, dating from around 800 BC or the early Iron Age.

This was an important lesson in the value of a close examination of the shape or form of vessels. Because our cup had a sloping shoulder and a small concave indentation up to the rim, Niall was able to define it as early Iron Age. This and other finds from Trench 3 meant that we were able to give a definitive date for the feature and extrapolate this evidence onto the other features that were found in the geophysics.

As the end of Day Three approached and we shared a drink of beer with the local community, we were able to say that we had found good evidence of another community that existed here in the Iron Age over 2,800 years ago. It seemed likely that this population had occupied the site for nearly 1,000 years and in the Roman period had created a large farmstead with an enclosure which had survived for the 400 years of the Roman occupation. So altogether, as Phil and Francis confirmed, this was nearly 1,500 years of occupation, which for three days of archaeology was not a bad return.

By working with the people of Caerau, we hope that we can stimulate interest in this marvellous monument that exists not far from their back doors. The enthusiasm of the local people and the families who came up to visit the site certainly suggested that this would be the case.

NAOMI

Now, I love digging and I love the Iron Age, so when the offer 'Would you like to come and dig an Iron Age hillfort?' arose, I didn't need to be asked twice! My disbelief and excitement grew as soon as I saw the sizeable hillfort on aerial photographs and particularly the LiDAR survey, which detected potential earlier ramparts, not visible from the air alone. This was such an impressive array of banks and ditches; a real feature of the landscape. With a site as visibly stunning as this, it was seemingly crying out to tell a story and reveal its past secrets. More ditches were visible from the geophysics, and the excitement about

ABOVE: *Naomi and Jimmy using a GPS system to check the location of finds.*

the potential of this site grew – where there are ditches, there are usually finds and dating evidence!

Very little was previously known about the site, due to a lack of excavation. With the extent and duration of occupation of the site unknown, the site's significance and importance was potentially huge. Our aim was to characterize the nature and date of the site. What was the extent of the archaeology? How long was the hillfort occupied for? My initial feelings on this site were 'all or nothing': that is, the interior of the hillfort might be stuffed with archaeological features and finds, or there could be nothing! So we were all keen to get going on this one.

The first trench was soon open and it was apparent that this site would not be giving up its secrets easily. The features shown on the geophysics were not very clear on the ground. With this type of 'brown on brown' archaeology, you can only pick out features by digging and feeling the differences.

With the geophysical data growing by the hour, a number of interesting features were being thrown up: ditches, roundhouses' gullies, post holes and even possibly some kilns! But with the site sat on clay, the definition of archaeological features was weak in some parts. At least there were features over which more trenches could be opened and investigated. The

next step would be to find datable artefacts, which would help to tie together the relationship between the archaeological features and give us an idea about the chronology of the site: when was it occupied and how long for?

Day Two soon rolled around and after a day and a half of digging, a very small abraded piece of pottery emerged! I believe it was Roman, and it was shortly followed by two pieces of medieval pottery. This was great in terms of giving an indication of the longevity of the site, but very frustrating from an Iron Age hillfort point of view!

Community involvement within *Time Team* sites is usual, from groups of schoolchildren and local volunteer archaeology groups to members of the public passing by. This site was no exception, with people of all ages getting involved. The local community literally lives in the shadow of this hillfort, so with this in mind and with such a feeling of community spirit, we all really wanted to excavate and discover the features and artefacts necessary to tell a story and bring this site to life!

By the end of Day Two, the latest geophysical results were showing up some fairly clear features: a ring ditch or gully, which would hopefully be Iron Age, finally. So Trench 3 (my lucky number) was opened and cleaned, making the features stand out quite well. Not for long, though, as rain made everything look messy again. Bad weather, ephemeral features and clay make for disheartened archaeologists! But at least a piece of in situ Iron Age pottery could be seen. Unimpressive to look at, maybe, but we were desperate for stratified finds. Without these, we could not date the features or the site.

At the beginning of Day Three, I decided to target a small, round feature – possibly a pit or post hole. It is common practice on an archaeological evaluation such as this to string out a section line across a feature and initially only excavate half of it (especially useful if you have a large feature such as a ditch to dig). This is to enable the measurement of the depth and edges of the feature and to see if it contains any artefacts or ecofacts (environmental remains).

ABOVE: *Paul showing the stunning pottery sherds to the cameras.*

Only ten minutes into this task, a piece of pottery started to emerge! It appeared to be made from a coarse fabric – a positive sign that this may be from an early period. With every movement of the trowel, the pottery fragment grew bigger.

Then two more pieces were uncovered and they clearly fitted together. The pottery specialist, Paul Blinkhorn, was called over on the radio and he confirmed it was early Iron Age. I couldn't believe it: finally what we were looking for! There were also fragments (which fitted together) of a saddle quern stone – a fantastic sign of agricultural activity.

I quickly switched to excavating with plastic clay-modelling tools, so as not to damage the fragile pottery still sticking out in the section. Within moments, fragments of a different vessel began to surface within the fill of this shallow post hole. This vessel had a lip or ledge at the shoulder. Unbelievably, it was of an earlier date: late Bronze Age. This was genuinely unexpected and news was soon buzzing around the site, much to the excitement of the local volunteers, schoolchildren and even the security guards! Even the local press came out. I think I was most excited of all: I am usually such an unlucky archaeologist when it comes to finding artefacts. It may not have been gold, or coins, but to me this was impressive – it made me do a little jig in the trench! It was soon agreed that the pottery vessels with the quern stone indicated that the site may even have had some ritual significance. The term 'ritual' is often overused, but even I agreed that the deposition of these objects in this context was a little odd. The decision was taken to extend the trench and dig the other half of the feature, but sadly there was no more to be found in it.

RIGHT: *A close-up of the early Iron Age pottery sherds.*

The sun was setting and after the whole team had gathered together to film the 'end of day' scene, I headed back to Trench 3 to tidy up and to ensure the precious pottery was correctly labelled and bagged. While I was doing so, a few of the teens from the community group asked for an explanation of the trench and the star finds. One of them was genuinely astonished by what we had found over the last three days, especially the finds from the post hole. He told me that his grandfather owned the land and he'd always played on the hillfort as a child and had no idea that such artefacts would be underground. For two and a half days Time Team had feared the same thing!

Before they left, they asked me, 'So as a reward for finding this, what do you get?' I replied that the reward for me and every archaeologist I've ever met is simply in the discovery of such finds, learning about them and ultimately sharing that knowledge with others. For me personally, the dissemination of archaeological information at any and every level is the most important thing.

And in that moment, I remembered why I had wanted a career in archaeology. Despite the difficult nature of the archaeology at this and many sites, it demonstrated how most archaeological sites really are. It shows how disappointment can turn to elation with the scrape of a trowel. Such a visibly impressive hillfort does not guarantee equally visible archaeological features beneath the soil. The features aren't always obvious and the finds are not always plentiful. But the speed at which knowledge about a site can change, and the way that a handful of pottery fragments can reveal so much about a site that was otherwise unknown, keeps you going in the wind and rain. It's what made me become an archaeologist in the first place.

RIGHT: *Naomi getting stuck into a trench at Caerau.*

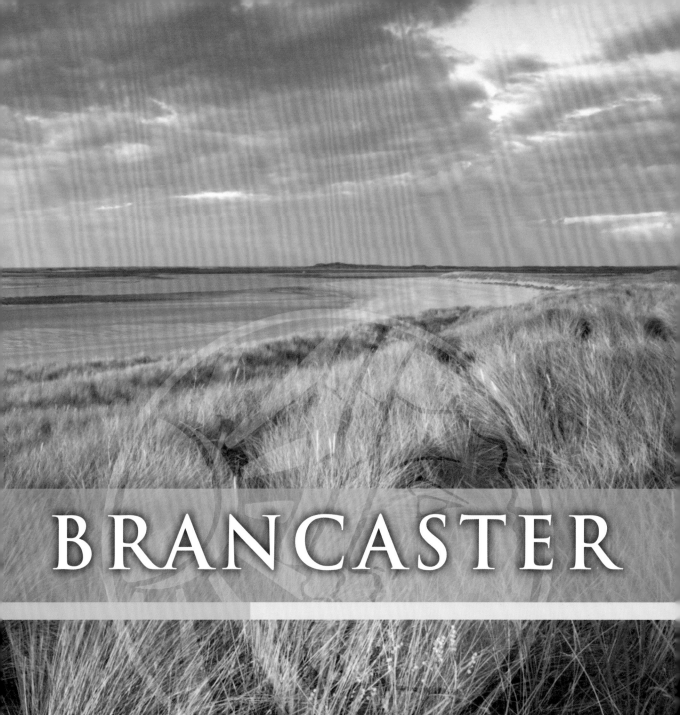

BRANCASTER

DAY ONE

Brancaster was yet another extraordinary site. It began with an amazing set of crop marks and was important because it featured a class of monument, the Saxon Shore Fort, that represents an iconic feature of Romano-British history.

THERE ARE ELEVEN of these forts stretching from East Anglia to the Isle of Wight, and it is arguable that their origins have very little to do with Saxons! They did function as a defensive ring around the coast of eastern Britain, but they also had a long history as Roman forts and centres of trade. The chance to look at one of these sites and take in both the fort itself and the town that surrounded it was a unique opportunity.

The importance of the site meant that at an early stage we had to get the support, advice and input from some of the key 'stakeholders', as Jim Mower, our development producer, refers to them. These people would be playing crucial roles over the three days of the shoot; in many ways this project was a great example of what collaborative, intelligent effort could achieve.

As Brancaster was a scheduled ancient monument, it was important to get English Heritage's approval, permission and support. Jim spent a lot of time talking to Dr Will Fletcher, the English Heritage inspector, and David Gurney, the local county archaeologist. David is a mine of information on these sites and has had a great deal of experience excavating Roman forts. The land is owned by the National Trust, so it was also important to work with Vicky Francis, the

ABOVE: *Francis and Tony checking out the first trench at Brancaster. If Francis looks anxious, that's because he was!*

National Trust coordinator for this area, and with the National Trust's chief archaeologist for Norfolk, Angus Wainwright.

Francis Pryor would be in charge of the archaeology. After a summer of torrential rain showers we were relieved to be blessed by good weather on the first day. Francis was fairly nervous about the site: we were taking on a huge area, and these are very important monuments, which typically throw up a wide range of complex issues.

As usual, the key goals had been hammered

out by Jim in consultation with all the relevant people and put into the project design. These were as follows:

Research aim 1: What is the character of the archaeology represented by crop marks at both the main fort site and the eastern vicus?

Research aim 2: What is the chronological sequence of fort construction at Brancaster? Is there a second-century fort at the site?

Research aim 3: Does any evidence survive for beachside development at Brancaster?

As usual, the project design defines the area we can excavate and the number of trenches we can dig. This is particularly important in the case of a scheduled ancient monument.

It is proposed that the precise location of invasive trenches will be based on the results of detailed topographical and geophysical survey and on-site discussion with relevant archaeological officers. A maximum area of 250 sq metres is proposed for invasive trenching to include up to eight individual trenches, unless further trenching is deemed appropriate and agreed to by representatives of English Heritage.

ABOVE: *Phil and Francis overlooking the first trench. Francis is not looking any happier!*

The television goal, as expressed in Tony's opening piece to camera, simplified the issues we would be facing at Brancaster.

This site was also going to be a big test of GSB's Advanced Radar System. In discussions with John and Jimmy, it became clear that one of

TONY'S PIECE TO CAMERA

 **❝** *I'm walking on what was once an ancient shoreline on the far west coast of Norfolk. If I'd have been here around 1,900 years ago, this area here would have been a beach and there'd be loads of Romans here. Now, they weren't working on their tan, they'd have been far too busy unloading cargo from ships to supply a massive fort that was just through here …*

And this site has a lot more: these crop marks show not only the fort but what appears to be a completely unexplored settlement to the east. There have been alluring finds made by locals already.

Could this site have been not only a defensive outpost but also a major trading centre with Roman Britain and even the Continent?

This is a 6-acre site we are about to dig. So can we uncover the story of 250 *years of Roman occupation here at Branodunum in just three days?* **❞**

the most fascinating aspects of the dig would be the degree to which the geophysical survey confirmed what the crop marks suggested and what the geophysics could uncover in some of the blank areas that lay within the fort itself. These forts were huge centres of administration, and it is likely that Brancaster had been in existence for 300–400 years. Warehouses, barrack blocks, granaries and administration buildings were all possibilities. We had on hand Mark Corney, *Time Team*'s Roman expert, to clarify what the main targets should be.

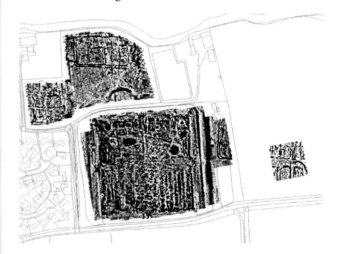

ABOVE: *The magnetometry played an important role at Brancaster. It was one of the largest surveys we have ever done on* Time Team.

With such a huge site, the key question for me on Day One was which building would be the most diagnostic and important in terms of phasing to excavate. Phasing in an archaeological context refers to the order of structures built on a site. The most diagnostic of these structures is the one that allows us to associate a specific date with a specific building. If, as we expected, John's geophysics produced a huge number of potential targets, we and all the assembled experts had got

MINI SKILLS MASTERCLASS

DIGGING AT SCHEDULED ANCIENT MONUMENTS

The site of the Roman fort at Brancaster is listed as a Scheduled Ancient Monument, or SAM. This meant that not only did we need to seek the permission of the landowner in order to excavate, but also from English Heritage. In the UK a SAM is defined as an archaeological site or historic building of national importance. Such remains are often valuable resources for research, tourism, education, leisure and local regeneration. However, they are also finite, irreplaceable and fragile resources that are highly vulnerable both to natural processes and to a range of human activities. For this reason they are protected under strict legislation and carrying out any activity at these sites without consent is a criminal offence.

There are approximately 20,000 SAMs in England. While large ruins are included, the majority are inconspicuous archaeological sites within fields, like the Brancaster site. A vast range of chronological and geographic sites are included as SAMs, from prehistoric settlements and burial mounds to twentieth-century military structures, and from the highest uplands to below the coastal tideline.

Under the Ancient Monuments and Archaeological Areas Act (1979), a SAM is protected against unauthorized change or unlicensed metal detecting. Therefore, if you wish to dig on such a site, written consent from the Secretary of State for Culture, Media and Sport is required before any archaeological work can be carried out. This includes excavation, but also geophysical surveys and various mapping techniques. English Heritage, Historic Scotland and CADW are the three governing bodies that protect and monitor all of the listed sites in

ABOVE: *Working alongside English Heritage inspectors like Will Fletcher is an important aspect of our work.*

Great Britain. Applications for consent should be submitted to the relevant governing body, who will then forward the application to the secretary of state, along with any recommendations as to whether consent should be given and, if so, any conditions that should be attached to the consent. It is advisable to contact the appropriate authority to discuss plans at an early stage before an application is made in order to identify the likelihood of a proposed scheme being granted consent in principle before any detailed project design is undertaken. To find out more, a document entitled *Scheduled Monuments* is available from the Department of Culture, Media and Sport's website.

to be sure that what we targeted would provide essential information to enable us to understand the monument.

From the start we had focused on three aspects of the fort's structure: the principal or main administration building, the main structural walls of the fort, and a feature which appeared to show a building that was out of alignment with the others and therefore possibly from an earlier structure (from an early stage this was referred to on the TV side as the 'squiffy' building). We were also keen to find information about the town, or vicus, which existed outside the fort. This was particularly important because there had been discussions about potential future buildings in the area and any information we could find would help English Heritage to respond accordingly.

From the very start we began to find huge amounts of Roman pottery in Trench 1, dug by Phil. This can be very distracting when you have a television crew around. Directors love to get the camera crew in and film whatever comes up,

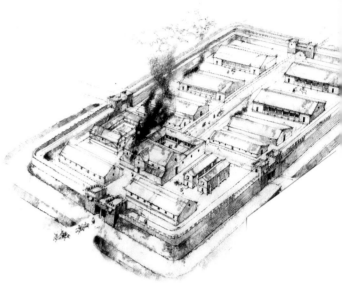

and of course while this is going on the digging stops and we lose valuable time. However, it soon became clear that in Phil's trench we had identifiable remnants of walls and large amounts of datable pottery.

As usual, the question in archaeology was whether we could find pottery that dated the construction of the walls. This would mean going

RIGHT: *Philippa Walton helping to identify our Roman pewter plate.*

ABOVE RIGHT: *Victor's drawing of a typical Roman fort with 'playing card' corners.*

WHAT ARE CROP MARKS?

Before we excavate anything on *Time Team*, a group of experts will head out into the field to have a careful look at both the planned excavation site and the surrounding landscape. This exercise is particularly important, as it is often the case that clues indicating the presence of subsurface archaeological features can easily be seen without using any technical equipment. Crop marks are a key indicator for archaeological remains, so the team get very excited when we find ones as clear as those present at Brancaster.

Crop marks are created through the differing growth rates and consequent colours of crops in certain areas within the field. A buried stone wall, for example, will create less moisture in the soil, and so the crops directly above it will be stunted compared to the rest of the field. An ancient ditch, on the other hand, filled with more organic matter than the surrounding soil, provides more nourishing conditions, meaning the crops directly above it will grow slightly quicker and taller than those surrounding them.

The clarity of crop marks is dependent on both the type of crop being grown and the local soil conditions. Wheat and oats are particularly sensitive to soil water content and therefore often show marks more clearly, while others, like grass and potatoes, are not so affected, making crop marks harder to detect. Similarly, crop marks are easier to spot in well-drained, sandy or chalky soils, rather than poorly drained clays.

The best way to see crop marks is from the air. When this isn't possible, aerial photographs can be of great help; these can sometimes be found within local and national archives. In the case of prominent features, it is also possible to view crop marks from high buildings or hills.

Picking the right time of day to view a field can also help identify crop marks. The best time is early or late in the day, when the sun is low in the sky and so very clear shadows due to crop height are visible.

During the autumn and winter months, when there are no crops in the field and the majority of fields have been ploughed, it is often still possible to identify archaeological features through soil marks rather than crop marks. Soil marks are differences in soil colour as a direct result of archaeological features. Depending on the geology of the area, soil marks may show up as white against brown (common in areas of clay) or brown against white (common in chalky areas). Highly organic or large burnt deposits may show up as black or even red. In all cases, knowledge of the local area and the judgements of archaeologists are essential in interpreting their significance.

ABOVE: *An example of crop marks at Nesley, Gloucestershire.*

BELOW: *A close-up of the stunning radar results. The principia is to the right and the potential granary bottom left.*

down deeper into the site to find the construction trench for the wall. As Trench 1 continued and Trench 2 was put in around the 'squiffy' building, the geophysics results continued to come in.

Our radar equipment was proving particularly useful at this site. Jimmy later explained its crucial role:

MALÅ's MIRA radar system, which we used at Brancaster, is the geophysics equivalent of upgrading to HDTV – well, almost! The system has many more antennae than a standard radar instrument and they are very closely spaced, which means that the level of detail that we can get from a survey is far greater. It worked brilliantly at Brancaster: we were confident that if there were buildings within the Roman enclosure, we'd have a good chance of getting some decent results, but only if the preservation and ground conditions played ball. As it was, the site was stuffed with buildings, the soils were good and the preservation excellent; the coming together of all these factors produced a stunning data set and the fact that we were using 'HD Radar' allowed us to pick out detail like the hypocaust systems, buttresses and column bases, as well as glimpses of early phases of building beneath the more prominent later examples. Despite all this, some people seemed to think the only reason we liked it was because we got to tow it around behind a buggy, rather than doing the old-fashioned legwork!

The Advanced Radar Unit was now in action. However, much to the amusement of the diggers and Phil, it was temporarily handicapped by a wheel falling off. While we waited for Jimmy to do running repairs and for the next set of results, the landscape archaeologists had a chance to consider Brancaster in its wider context.

In the Roman period, Brancaster was known as Branodunum and was important enough in the fourth century to be mentioned in the *Notitia Dignitatum* – the list of Roman civil and military officials. The reason for its location is by no means clear. There are no major roads or large waterways connecting it to the hinterland, nor is there an obvious harbour. David Gurney was keen to look for the fort's origin as a centre of trade and commerce. There is also confusion concerning the description of these monuments as Saxon Shore Forts. This term, which was first used by the Romans, could imply sites acting as a defence against the Saxons or possibly settled by the Saxons. One of the features of the site referred to by antiquarians was the large amount of pale stone used in the construction of the walls.

To the east and west of the fort the crop marks had shown two settlement areas usually referred to by the Roman term *vicus*. In the 1970s an archaeological dig had taken place in the settlement to the west and this had produced many finds, including a gold ring possibly owned

LEFT: *The Roman gaming piece.*

by the Commander of Branodunum that may have been used as a seal. This has been dated from AD 270–274 because it shows the bust of an emperor thought to be Tetricus.

At the end of Day One, Tracey uncovered one of the best finds of the day: a Roman die. The trenches continued to produce huge amounts of pottery and other finds, and it had become clear that Wessex Archaeology and all the team processing pots, including volunteers from the *Time Team* Academy, were going to have their work cut out for them. It was only 4 o'clock on Day One and we already had several trays of pottery, bone, oyster shell from a wide range of Roman periods. Could we find the critical pieces that would date the structure on Day Two?

LEFT: *The large array of finds from just two days' work at Brancaster.*

ROMAN POTTERY

Pottery is a common find on excavated Roman sites such as Brancaster, since pottery was produced in such vast quantities across the Roman Empire. Generally, Roman domestic pottery is divided into two broad categories: coarse wares and fine wares. The former category comprises the everyday dishes, bowls and jars used for storage and transportation, and in some cases tableware. Fine wares, on the other hand, were generally serving vessels or tableware used for more formal occasions and were usually more elegant and decorative.

Coarse wares

The term coarse wares covers a huge variety of vessels, but within this broad group there are three important categories: amphorae, cooking pots and mortaria. Amphorae or amphoras were storage vessels used to transport food on both long and short journeys. The content was often liquid, commonly olive oil or wine, but sometimes garum – a popular fish and fruit sauce. Amphorae were usually two-handled with a cylindrical or globular body and often exhibited a spiked base. This ingenious design allowed the containers to be tightly packed onto ships and made them convenient for handling once they reached their destination.

The second category, cooking pots, were simple functional earthenware bowls, a standard item within every kitchen during the Roman period. Because the geographical span is so vast, Roman cooking pots are studied on a regional basis. A common type found within the British Isles is black burnished ware, first made in the south-west of England during the late Iron Age, though it enjoyed continued popularity throughout the Roman period, where it was

ABOVE: *A small collection of pottery finds, including black burnished ware in the centre.*

made in greater quantities and marketed more widely.

Unlike black-burnished ware, the mortarium is a vessel type closely linked with the spread of Roman culture and cuisine. The mortarium is a shallow bowl with a thick rim curving outwards, making it easy to handle, and often a pouring lip. The internal surface was deliberately roughened with a coating of grit or coarse sand during manufacture. It appears the vessel was used in a similar manner to a pestle and mortar in order to grind ingredients with which to season dishes. Interestingly, within Britain the first mortarium found had been imported from Gaulish sources more than a decade before Britain became a Roman province, showing a growing influence of Roman culture in the late pre-Roman Iron Age.

Fine wares

The second broad group, fine wares, is a term used by archaeologists to describe pottery that was intended to be used for serving food and drink at the table. Again, many different types exist, from pottery finished with enamel or lead glazes to very delicate, thin-walled drinking vessels. However, perhaps the most well-known are the red-gloss wares of Italy and Gaul, traditionally known as *terra sigillata* (literally sealed or slipped clay) or, as it is often referred to by British archaeologists, samian ware. These vessels were widely traded from the first century BC to the late second century AD, and they have become synonymous with the Roman Empire as a result of their frequent appearance on Roman archaeological sites.

Samian-ware vessels are well fired, meaning they are fairly hard. They have a glossy surface of hues ranging from light orange to bright red. Manufacture often took place in large warehouse complexes along industrial lines, thus creating a highly standardized product.

See pages 60–1 for more examples of Roman pottery.

BELOW: *An example of samian ware, showing two figures believed to be boxers. Note the site reference number on the plastic bag.*

As with many Roman sites, much of the stone from the buildings at Brancaster had been stolen; it had suffered from the attentions of a local vicar referred to by Francis as 'The Robbing Reverend'.

ABOVE: *Phil showing Tony a selection of finds from Trench 1.*

OVERNIGHT WE HAD been able to review some of the finds including the die and a large pewter bowl from Phil's trench, which Philippa Walton from the British Museum identified as Roman fourth century. These are very rare finds: Philippa pointed out that it was the first pewter vessel from an excavation that she had ever held.

At the beginning of Day Two, it was decided to place a trench across the seaward defences of the fort. Francis wanted a good large trench, which would give us the chance of possibly finding the foundations of the fort walls. Raksha was in charge of this trench and soon began to find pieces of grey stone – the remnants of the material that clad the walls of the fort. What

would be important in Trench 3 would be to find material that would specifically date when these walls were built.

Back in Phil's trench, Roman finds were still appearing in large numbers. Tracey had uncovered an iron stylus used to inscribe a wax tablet. This was identified by Mark Corney: as he put it, this was 'nice evidence of Roman Army bureaucracy in action'.

To the west of the fort, the 1970s excavations had also unearthed a number of Roman military finds. These included tiles stamped with 'CHIAQ', which Mark identified as the first cohort of Aquitanians from south-west France, who were likely to have been involved at the early stages of the fort in the first century. One of *Time Team*'s earliest shoots was at Ribchester, where one of the Roman experts made the point that most of the construction of these early forts was done by the legions themselves. They had to be both fighters and builders and were trained to dig while fully suited in armour. By the fourth century at Brancaster, we have a reference to a cavalry regiment of Dalmatians in the *Notitia Dignitatum*, illustrating both the importance of cavalry to the Romans and their use of soldiers from throughout Europe.

One of the advantages of having a small finds expert like Philippa on a site is that we are able to identify, record and if necessary conserve small metal finds as they actually appear. *Time Team* usually works with local metal detectorists in

consultation with the local finds liaison officer (FLO). This kind of work has become very important with the increasing interest in metal detecting (see masterclass on page 50).

We were finding increasingly large numbers of coins and it was great to be able to get a relatively instant diagnosis from Philippa. One of the coins from Raksha's trench showed a soldier spearing a fallen horseman on one side and the head of Roman Emperor Julian II on the other. Philippa was able to date this as having been minted between AD 355 and 361. Small coins are a relatively common find on large Roman sites; see the masterclass on page 50 for more information on how they are cleaned and conserved.

On Day Two we were able to get a wider perspective of the coastline, with Tony taking a trip with David Gurney to look at the site from the coast. The sea would have been a lot closer to our fort in the fourth century, and typically the

WHAT DOES A FINDS LIAISON OFFICER DO?

The role of a finds liaison officer (FLO) is to record any archaeological find discovered by the general public. It is vital that the finds themselves and the location in which they are found are recorded; if not, it is almost as if they never existed. When a new find is brought to us, we measure, weigh, photograph and write a description of the artefact. All of this information is then entered into our database for the benefit of researchers, other archaeologists, local historians and future generations.

Chronologically, we record anything from the Palaeolithic era to around the eighteenth century. We receive finds from a huge variety of people, although the main group we deal with are metal detectorists, some of whom are independent, although many belong to clubs. Officers stay in regular contact with metal detectorists in order to help record the large amount of material they collect. As a result, we record a lot of metal, although a vast assortment of other artefacts are also brought to us by the general public, from prehistoric flints and axe heads to Roman artefacts like coins and tiles, and even medieval objects such as pottery, brooches and belts. If you find any artefact yourself, the advice will always be to consult with your local finds liaison officer.

Anyone who finds an artefact can bring it to us for identification and recording, and no find is too small or insignificant: even a tiny piece of ancient flint can form part of a larger picture, which may help us to identify new archaeological sites. To contact your local finds liaison officer or find out more about our work, please visit our website: www.finds.org

Cleaning Roman coins

People will often try to clean artefacts such as coins after finding them. I have seen Roman coins dipped in wax, boot polish or even high-grade cleaning products, which can absolutely ruin the coin; this is particularly sad when a coin has survived for over 2,000 years within the ground. It is all right to gently remove the mud; but you should not do anything else until you have shown it to a professional archaeologist. Our catchphrase is 'ABC', which stands for: Advice Before Cleaning.

Danni Wootton

ABOVE: *Philippa Walton from the British Museum was our finds liaison officer at Brancaster.*

Romans used flat-bottomed boats which could be beached on a high tide. *Time Team* had discovered a very similar boat in an excavation in Holland broadcast in 2006. These boats can carry considerable loads. We asked Victor to reconstruct the scene as it might have looked at the end of the fourth century.

As Raksha began to find more and more grey stone, it was clear that the amount needed to clad a fort with walls 5 or 6 metres high would have been considerable. Experts have identified the stone as coming from Castle Rising, and it has been estimated that it would have taken over 500 boatloads to get enough of it to the site. After the decline of the fort much of this stone was stolen and found its way into local buildings, including the churches; to see it high up in these structures gives us a good idea of how impressive this fort would have looked from the distance.

In Raksha's rampart trench she was beginning to get an idea of how wide the foundations might have been. She had been able to locate the edges, which were over 3½ metres (10 ft) apart.

As Day Two progressed we were getting more and more results from the geophysics and in particular the radar, which indicated that in Phil's trench there was a large underground chamber in the centre of the principal building. Mark Corney potentially regarded this as a sacrum – the treasure house of the main headquarters building.

BELOW: *Victor's picture of boats moored along the coastline at Brancaster.*

RIGHT: *A wide selection of animal bones were found at the site, many of which showed signs of butchering.*

Between the fort and the coast there was a large field that also had crop marks and John's latest set of magnetometry indicated a complex of ditches and road systems. Could this potentially be an earlier fort? Both Francis and David were keen to excavate one of the ditches to see if dating material could be found.

During the afternoon of Day Two we asked Naomi Sewpaul to look at all of the bone material that was coming from the site. She was able to make an on-the-spot analysis, which gave us an idea of the range of food being eaten in the fort. Cow, sheep and pig bone were present and many had clear butchery marks from both cleavers and small knives. In addition to the bones we also had a collection of cock spurs, which possibly indicated that cock fighting was going on as a pastime in the fort.

On the theme of food and cooking, Mark was

able to give us an overview of a typical selection of Roman pottery, including mortaria – large bowls with grit embedded in the surface which enables food to be processed. There was a wide range of domestic pottery and some large items of high-status samian ware on which food would have been served.

It is interesting to note that for the Romans, pork was a delicacy: the large number of pig bones showed that at various times the soldiers had been living fairly well. At the end of Day Two

LEFT: *Graeme Attwood on his way to completing over 8 hectares (20 acres) of magnetometry!*

we were able to enjoy a range of Roman food spiced with coriander and fenugreek and cooked with garam sauce made from decomposed fish.

A final visit to Ian and David's trench on what we hoped would be an earlier phase of the fort produced some critical evidence. In the fill of the ditch, well stratified, were pieces of first- and second-century BC Iron Age pottery. This could be identified by the flint inclusions. If our work on the final day turned up no Roman material in these trenches, it was beginning to look as though the Roman fort at Branodunum had been preceded by an Iron Age settlement.

A close-up of a Roman pewter dish.

HOW TO TELL THE DIFFERENCE BETWEEN ANIMAL AND HUMAN BONE

There is so much that the study of bone from both animals and humans can tell us. As an archaeozoologist, I deal with animals from a variety of species, which come in a variety of shapes and sizes. But I am often asked: 'How can you tell the difference between animal and human bone?' My initial reaction is always to smile! This is because despite bone being of the same composition in both animals and humans, to me personally, human bone physically feels different. It's like having a weird sixth sense, or a rubbish superpower!

Despite this 'sense' having never let me down thus far, there is a far more scientific and methodical way of doing things which I always employ. Unless it is quite obvious that you have in front of you an entire animal or human skeleton, animal and human bone may at first glance look the same. Human bone often gets mixed up amid contexts of animal bone, for example at rubbish pits or ditch deposits. Accidents will have happened in the past as they do today, so it is not uncommon to find a human finger bone among the kitchen waste! The remains of human infants are also commonly mistaken for animal bone, particularly that of young animals, due to their size, shape and porous nature. Ribs of young children also closely resemble those of a small and/or young animal, making identification extremely difficult (a second or third opinion would be advisable).

When presented with any kind of bone, there are three general levels of identification, which can be used in every case to determine whether bone derives from a human or an animal.

ABOVE: *Exposing a finger bone.*

- Gross anatomy/bone macrostructure, or identification with the naked eye. Which bone is it? Where in the body is it from? What are its special anatomical features?
- Are there any surface alterations, such as burning or butchery, for example? For the most part, burning and butchery will occur on animal bone, but humans are not fully exempt from this.
- Bone microstructure. If the bone is very small, fragmented or eroded, examination under the microscope can help determine the species, as the microscopic structure of bone differs between animals and humans.

Animal and human skeletons are comprised mostly of the same elements: femur, tibia, humerus and so forth. These elements will look similar to each other from species to species and share similar characteristics. However, many of the anatomical differences between species are related to functional morphology: that is, how a particular species moves and adapts to its particular environment. For example, the leg bones of a horse or deer are more elongated and gracefully slender (or gracile), designed for running, compared with those of a mole, whose forelimbs are short and powerful, designed for digging.

Bone identification checklist

All bone finds should be examined with the aid of an anatomical reference collection, supplementary identification manuals and expert opinion where possible, especially in the case of very fragmented or young bone. Below are some of the key points that help to identify the differences between human and animal bone.

Cranium and mandible (head and jaw)

- Human and animal skulls look very different. Skulls are more fragile than other parts of the body (in both humans and animals) and archaeologically are generally preserved in a fragmented way. Humans have a large cranial vault and a small face; the opposite is true for animals.
- Human eyes are positioned facing forward; animal eyes are generally at the sides.
- Humans have a chin; this feature is absent in animals.
- U-shaped jaw in humans; V-shaped jaw in animals.

ABOVE: *A close-up of teeth from a jaw bone found at Barrow Clump.*

Dentition (teeth)

- Human (omnivorous): teeth reflect a generalized design, with a mix of incisors (for slicing), canines (for puncturing) and molars (for grinding).
- Human teeth are more rounded in general than animal teeth. Animal teeth reflect specialized dietary adaptations for that particular species: herbivorous grazers, carnivorous shredders and so on.
- Different numbers of teeth for different species. The mouth is divided into four, or quadrants, with each quadrant comprising the following: Human – 2 (incisors), 1 (canine), 2 (premolars), 3 (molars); Animal – 3 (incisors), 1 (canine), 4 (premolars), 3 (molars).

Post-cranial bones (bones not of the skull)

- These are the long bones: femur, tibia, humerus, spine and so forth. As mentioned above, they are the size and shape they are for a particular species based on patterns of locomotion or functional morphology – how they move.
- Human forelimbs are less robust than those of animals.
- Animal bones have a greater density relative to the animal's size: they are less porous and thicker in cross-section than those of humans. The thickness of animal cortical (outer bone) is greater than in humans.
- Bowl-shaped pelvis in humans; narrow, long pelvis in animals.
- The femur in humans is the longest bone in the body. In animals it is similar in length to other long bones, such as the tibia or humerus.
- Humans bear weight mostly on the heel and toes, resulting in a long, narrow foot. Animals bear weight mostly on their toes, resulting in a broader foot.

Naomi Sewpaul

At the end of Day Two, one of Jimmy's radar plots had shown what appeared to be a potential granary and a strange elliptically shaped area.

RIGHT: *Francis talking through tactics with county archaeologist David Gurney and Roman expert Mark Corney. They were about to make a critical decision.*

THERE WAS A lot of talk about digging one final trench on our final day at the site. The push for 'one last trench' has over the last twenty years often produced a critical last-minute answer at a dig. At Brancaster I felt it was important for us to do it: I wanted something that would introduce an element of spontaneity and present a real challenge to the team. To continue working on the trenches we'd opened on the first two days would enable us to work on some important finds in detail, but it would present no strategic challenge.

I had suggested to the team that we would have enough manpower to open one last trench, based on the geophysics findings that seemed to suggest either a granary or a Roman *gyrus* – a circular structure thought to be used for training cavalry horses. There seemed to be some enthusiasm for another trench; Mark Corney, one of our Roman experts, pointed out that a small trench could confirm the existence of buttresses – a distinctive feature of a granary. Francis seemed to have agreed to this plan at the end of Day Two, although I was aware that we would be stretching our resources.

Over the years on *Time Team* we have consistently provided extra labour on the fourth and fifth days to cover backfilling and recording.

This has allowed us to extend our work right up to the end of Day Three. However, this would not be happening at Brancaster. Day Three began with Francis, having thought things through overnight, deciding that one last trench would be a trench too far. Over the years, the arrangement I had arrived at with Mick was that if he felt the archaeology was overstretched, he could veto a final trench. To give Mick, Francis and our other team leaders their due, they have shared a perception that *Time Team* is about achieving a balance between archaeology and TV, and sometimes they have been prepared to go beyond their comfort zone if I made a good case based on the availability of labour and the advice of experts.

ABOVE: *Finds from previous excavations at Brancaster include this beautiful gold ring.*

At Brancaster, Francis believed we already had too much work to do on the finds emerging from the existing trenches. I also felt that the size of the operation we were running had put more pressure on him, and I accepted his decision. Given that I have probably been trying the patience of archaeologists for twenty years, it might have been a piece of poetic justice for them to have the final say in what may well turn out to be the final *Time Team* in its present form!

Early on Day Three we were getting more and more results from the radar indicating an underground cellar beneath the centre of the principia. Phil had actually begun to uncover beautifully shaped stones in his trench, and the backfilling of sand suggested that this might be an area where we could locate fresh Roman finds that hadn't been disturbed by people taking building material from the site.

RAKSHA

Day Three for me was one of the most important breakthroughs of the shoot. As an archaeologist, you always hope that the question the trench has been designed to answer will be answered by the evidence that we find. The major breakthrough was the discovery of the earthen rampart, which proved to be from an early fort and was crucially on a different alignment from the fort walls.

In the trenches we were able to see how the stone fort had been cut into this early rampart – a detail that only excavation could have given us. We therefore had two phases of fort on slightly different alignments, and it is always satisfying as an archaeologist to get a sense of the chronological order of things. Francis was definitely very chuffed!

My favourite find from all the material that we uncovered was the small cube of white stonework that was a remnant of the material used to make the main walls. There was enough of it for us to imagine what these walls might have looked like when they were originally built.

One of the main challenges on a site like this for the diggers is distinguishing between material that has been re-deposited due to the action of later disturbance and material that is associated with the first phase of construction of the fort itself.

Digging on these huge foundations made me wonder what the gatehouse might have looked like; I had an image in my mind of the reconstructed gatehouse at Verulamium. A gatehouse built in the stone that we were finding with the light shining on it would have been a real landmark for Roman sailors approaching the fort and possibly a warning to invaders thinking of attacking.

LEFT: *Raksha briefing Francis about the discovery of the earthen ramparts.*

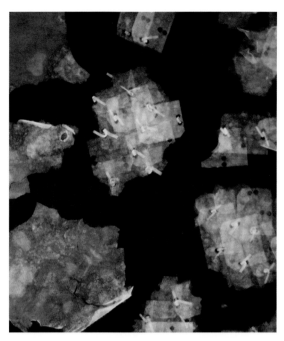

ABOVE: *An X-ray of a fragment of Roman armour found in the basement of the sacrum.*

distance every day with the magnetometer, was getting close to completing a scan of the entire site. This would mean that John, Jimmy, Emma and Graeme had completed one of the largest scans ever done on *Time Team*: approximately 22 acres in all.

The conclusions we were able to draw more than answered the questions that had been set in the project design. According to David Gurney we had made a significant contribution to our understanding of Saxon Shore Forts. He was kind enough to send the following email a couple of weeks after the shoot had finished:

It is not an exaggeration when I say that the project has exceeded my expectations by a very long way, that the results of just three days' fieldwork, especially the geophysics, were amazing, and that in the thirty years I've been involved in Roman Norfolk those three days proved to be amongst the most exhilarating and productive. I wouldn't have missed it for anything!
There's no doubt that as a result of this we'll be able to rewrite the history of Roman Brancaster, make a major contribution to the archaeology of the Saxon Shore and, in due course, to greatly enhance the visitor experience and appreciation of the fort by local communities and visitors.

The sacrum was often used to keep money and other valuable objects safe, and it seemed possible that we might be able to get to its lower levels by the end of the day. With just three or four hours to go, Phil made a significant find: a collection of bronze pieces that looked like a set of small tongues. These were identified by Mark Corney as Roman armour or Lorica Squamata. These small pieces of bronze were sewn onto a leather or linen jerkin and dated from the third century. They were particularly related to sites where cavalry regiments were stationed.

By the afternoon of Day Three, Jimmy had collected so much data that the GPS which provided the location of each scan was beginning to crash. However, while he was sorting this out we were still able to collect mag data, and Graeme Attwood, who had been covering a huge

It was particularly important that we were able to show that the settlement to the north between the fort and the sea was actually Iron Age and had existed and thrived before the arrival of the Romans. As Tony put it nicely in his final piece to camera: these people must one day have looked up and perhaps seen the Roman ships arriving and 'from then on their lives were never the same again'. A somewhat fitting epitaph to our own work at Branodunum.

ROMAN POTTERY: 43 AD–410 AD
Some typical examples and how to identify them

1. Amphorae

Amphorae were large wheel-thrown terracotta containers, characterized by their narrow necks, pointed bases and the two handles from which their name is derived. Their peculiar shape allowed them to be tightly stacked on ships, facilitating their use as the transport containers of the Graeco-Roman world. The pointed base of an amphora also allowed it to be stored vertically in sand or soft ground once on land. Although predominantly used for the storage and transportation of olive oil and wine, numerous examples have been discovered on shipwrecks which indicate their use for myriad products, from fish sauce to the ashes of the dead.

2. South Gaulish samian ware

South Gaulish samian ware is a derivative of *terra sigillata*, a type of fine ware made within the regions of Italy and Gaul during the Roman Empire. *Terra sigillata* ware is characterized by its bright red to pale orange colour range and its glossy surface slips. Such items were mass produced and widely exported. South Gaulish samian ware, produced in several southern French cities, is distinguished from its Italian counterpart by the redder slip and pink fabric. A large proportion of vessels discovered exhibit decorative designs of vine scrolls and the occasional animal. Many examples are distinguished by their Dragendorff numbers, a classic type being Dragendorff 29, with its angular bowl.

3. Black burnished ware

Black burnished ware is a type of coarse ware that would have been used for cooking. The industry operated around the Poole Harbour area, and it is thought that these sand-tempered vessels are the direct successors of Iron Age pottery. The characteristic black colouring was created artificially by means of reduction firing: the sherds would be starved of oxygen during the final stages of the firing process, ordinarily using a damp material heaped over the bonfire. Such was the consistency of their appearance that these wares were originally believed to have been wheel-thrown; however, it was discovered in the late 1960s that this huge industry was, remarkably, entirely handmade.

4. Mortaria

A mortarium (plural mortaria) was a kitchen vessel, used predominantly with a pestle for the grinding of herbs and spices, which is thought to be a characteristically Roman means of preparing food. Examples have been found in Britain dating from before the Roman conquest. This indicates that, as the result of trade or immigration, Roman-style cuisine was being enjoyed in Britain; similarly British aristocrats were known to have eagerly imported wine from the Roman Empire. These conically shaped vessels are characterized by a thick flange and the grits embedded into the inner bowl: there are signs that the inner bowl has been repetitively scraped and pounded during use. On some earlier Roman examples, potters have stamped their trademark on the vessels, which helps us to map the origin of these pots.

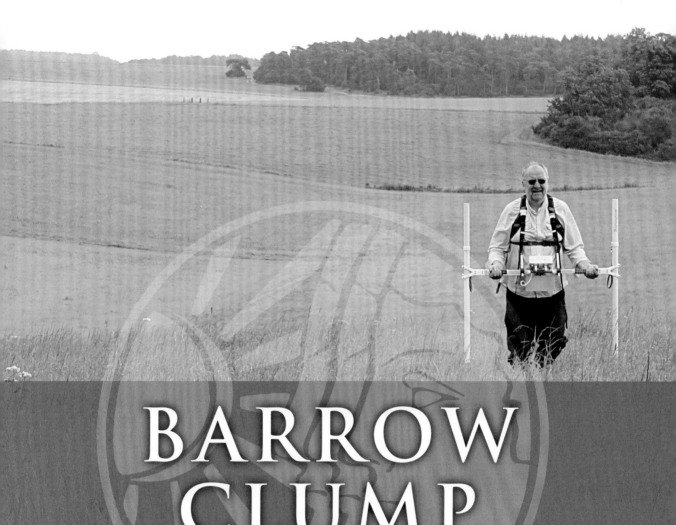

BARROW
CLUMP

Barrow Clump is the site of a group of Bronze Age barrows in Wiltshire, within the Salisbury Plain Ministry of Defence training ground.

LEFT: *Jimmy and Emma surveying the first grids.*

RIGHT: *Phil in the trench that would eventually transect the barrow.*

THE BARROWS FIRST came to light after archaeologists became aware of fragments of human bone and Anglo-Saxon metalwork appearing in the spoil from badger sets. There are many archaeological sites in Britain that have been heavily damaged by badgers. Resolving them often involves some very difficult discussions between archaeologists and groups wanting to protect badger populations. It often seems to me that the latter are possibly better organized and certainly capable of shouting louder than those who campaign to preserve our heritage. I have visited a number of important sites and witnessed the huge holes drilled through Roman buildings, ancient burials and other archaeology, all examples of a finite

resource that, once lost, can never be recovered. A healthy population of badgers, on the other hand, can withstand a degree of disturbance and have proved themselves adept at adapting to living alongside human beings over the years. Our heritage, once lost, is lost forever. It is important at these critical archaeological sites to find a solution that resolves the interests of both heritage and wildlife.

Evaluation of the site at Barrow Clump began in 2003, and some initial trenches revealed Anglo-Saxon burials with grave goods. Because of its proximity to the Salisbury Plain military training area, the project came under the control of the MoD archaeologist, Richard Osgood. At an early stage it was suggested that the site would be ideal for Operation Nightingale, an MoD scheme which uses archaeology as a tool in the rehabilitation of wounded and traumatized soldiers, particularly those coming home from recent conflicts in Afghanistan. Sergeant Diarmaid Walshe, of the First Battalion Rifles, who also has a background in archaeology, became a key coordinator of the project.

OPERATION NIGHTINGALE

The idea for Operation Nightingale came from Sergeant Walshe, who was the medical sergeant attached to 1st Battalion, The Rifles, at the time. He contacted me to say that one of the soldiers he was responsible for was a *Time Team* fanatic and really into archaeology, and he asked me if I thought archaeology would be a good method for recovery? I thought it would be perfect, as archaeology works so well for many people: it's out in the open air, working as a team, a social activity as well as using both your mind and your physical attributes.

So we set something up at Chisenbury Midden, a 700 BC late Bronze Age, early Iron Age site. Here the guys began to learn surveying and section-drawing skills, and that went really well, so we did another of those programmes. From that point we have looked for archaeological projects that the MoD wants to undertake but doesn't have the funds or resources to pursue. We also have tried to look for sites that would seem engaging and interesting to people entering the project. A variety of sites have been worked on, including a Roman villa site in Caerwent in Wales, and a Second World War Stirling bomber crash site. Eventually we wanted to have a big project that we could employ a lot of people on to work over the summer, which is why we chose Barrow Clump. This site is also on the Heritage at Risk Register, another really good reason for doing the project.

Of course, archaeology and the military have a real symbiotic relationship: people like Sir Mortimer Wheeler and Augustus Pitt Rivers both had a military background and an interest in archaeology, and over the course of the project we have come across many guys who have a degree in archaeology. There seems to be a real disciplinary crossover between archaeology and the military. Additionally, the guys working on this site are digging up warriors, with weapons and drinking vessels: in a sense it's their clan. There is a real connection and a sense of immediacy in recognizing the objects and their uses. We're hoping to complete this site within three years, when it will then be taken off the Heritage at Risk Register and the badgers can have it back.

Richard Osgood, Senior Historic Advisor, Defence Infrastructure Organization

ABOVE: *Jimmy showing the geophysics results to one of the service personnel.*

ABOVE: *Dinnertime at the site. Sergeant Diarmaid Walshe, our main contact with Operation Nightingale, stands by while the* Time Team *diggers are the first in line to be served!*

It is important to emphasize that this project is totally voluntary; we don't force anyone to take part – it just wouldn't be effective. Some service personnel accept the offer and some don't, but everyone who has participated has had a positive experience and it has helped with their recovery process. The key is that we do lots of different activities, from digging and surveying to photography and processing finds. Then in the evening there are activities including quizzes, talks and sporting events. The majority of service personnel here are still serving; two weeks is the minimum time people can come for, although most stay the entire six weeks.

There is a broad spectrum of injuries here: gunshot wounds, double amputees, serious arm injuries and psychological trauma. What we're doing is not a medical treatment: we describe it as a recovery activity – we give people something useful to do, which can help rebuild their self-esteem. A lot of these guys have been off sick for a long time, which can make them feel as though they have no real purpose any more. We feel it is vital to get their brains working again and give them something positive to strive for. One of the missions of the armed forces is to protect our sovereignty, our heritage and our identity, which is exactly what we're doing here, just in a slightly different way. We're particularly proud that as a result of this project some service personnel are now studying for degrees in archaeology and history at the University of Leicester.

Sergeant Diarmaid Walshe

ABOVE: *Working on the burials in the centre of the mound. This area represents about a quarter of the space excavated.*

On Day One Tony asked Diarmaid what kinds of trauma the soldiers had suffered. He explained: 'Some of them are physically injured, and we have amputees, guys who are blind or deaf, but most of them are suffering with the effects of war you can't always see – post-traumatic stress caused by death and suffering on an unimaginable scale that they witnessed.'

Part of the inspiration for Operation Nightingale was Corporal Steve Winterton. We were able to interview Steve on the first day. Badly injured in 2009 and requiring major reconstruction surgery on both legs, he no longer had a career in the army. His wife was afraid that he might commit suicide; for months he refused to leave the house, suffering panic attacks and losing interest in everything around him. Some strange trick of fate led him to start watching *Time Team* on television, and there was

something about the show that began to give him a focus. In his own words, he watched the programmes 'incessantly'. Along with the support of the army and his family, he began to turn his life around. Working with fellow soldiers on an archaeology site became his way of recovering. Today he is doing a degree in archaeology and ancient history at Leicester University and has enough confidence to give talks in front of huge crowds of people wanting to know more about the work of Operation Nightingale.

Working with the MoD, Wessex Archaeology, English Nature and Natural England, Operation Nightingale aimed to excavate the majority of the mound over three seasons. When *Time Team* arrived in 2012, during the first season, large numbers of burials were coming to light.

A key question we were asked to help answer related to the archaeology on the north side of the mound, an area that had still to be fully evaluated. Would it be possible to place a large trench across this area to characterize the archaeological evidence? Operation Nightingale were also keen to use John's geophysics to see if there were any other burial sites in the vicinity. As usual Tony's piece to camera simplified the key goals.

At the start of Day One, Richard Osgood and Diarmaid Walshe were on hand with a plan of the site showing the latest burials. These had included incredible examples of grave goods, such as amber beads, brooches and shield bosses. Richard pointed out that with the badgers destroying the archaeology, they needed to move quickly to excavate and record the site so that the information could be preserved and the badgers

left in peace. The main goals were to find out who was buried in the mound and when, and how big the cemetery was and how it was divided up.

The project design, prepared in close collaboration with the MoD, set out our main research aims.

ABOVE: *John pulling the advanced MALÅ radar machine. Conditions were not ideal.*

BELOW: *Helen and Tony discussing the finds emerging from one of the burials.*

TONY'S PIECE TO CAMERA

" Hidden amid these trees is an Anglo-Saxon site stuffed full of unbelievable treasures …

Barrow Clump was once a huge burial mound, where warriors and their families were laid to rest with all their riches.

Now a new set of warriors face a race against time to excavate the site before it's destroyed by the local wildlife.

For three days, Time Team is going territorial: joining forces with a team of soldiers to get to the bottom of this site. We'll be helping them piece together the size of the site and discovering who was buried here, when and why. "

Research aim 1: To excavate a specific trench designed to establish the condition of the unexplored half of the site, and whether the burials extend in that direction.

Research aim 2: To conduct geophysics in an area around the barrow to discover the extent of the site and burial ground.

As Phil pointed out, Barrow Clump began as a Bronze Age burial mound, perhaps as early as 3,000 BC, and was later reused by the Saxons, who made a habit of choosing ancient monuments for their burials. Richard told us that Roman pottery had also been found along with flints and other Neolithic material, which cheered Phil up considerably!

Trench 1 would be 20 metres long, examining the north side of the mound that had still to be evaluated. It would be, as Tony put it, 'a window

BELOW: *Richard Osgood talking archaeological tactics with Phil and Tony. Richard played a key role in the archaeological management of the site.*

BELOW: *Victor's illustration of a typical Anglo-Saxon burial from an earlier* Time Team *programme.*

into unchartered territory', effectively creating a time slice through the whole monument.

We planned to put Rob and Cassie into a second trench, where they would be working with the soldiers on a newly exposed grave cut. We had invited Helen Geake, *Time Team*'s Anglo-Saxon expert, to join us, and on the first day she had the delightful task of looking at some of the grave goods discovered during previous excavations. Helen observed that the burials had clearly included men, women and children. Alongside the knives and spearheads, there were beautiful beads and personal objects related to adornment and beauty. We have excavated Anglo-Saxon graves before and it seems likely that laying out burials with these beautiful brooches and beads was a way of expressing the wealth and status people had acquired over their

lifetimes. It is almost a public celebration of a life lived. To Helen, the finds at Barrow Clump suggested a high-status community of women warriors. By looking at the range of finds, she hoped to piece together a hierarchy of burial which might enable us to suggest whether or not the mound was divided by social status.

Jackie McKinley, *Time Team*'s bone specialist, was on hand to work on some specific skeletons, and we were able to watch as she began working on one of the key burials.

RIGHT: *Helen Geake working out the arrangement of burials around the mound.*

HOW TO EXCAVATE A BARROW

Barrows, burial mounds or tumuli are mounds of earth and/or stone placed over one or more graves, occasionally within a surrounding ring ditch. They often sit in very prominent places within the landscape, such as on hilltops or ridge lines. Many of these barrow sites have proved to be rich in grave goods, indicating that they may have contained the remains of tribal leaders or chieftains. However, excavations on some earthen long barrows have uncovered a complete lack of human remains, perhaps because these monuments may have been filling the role of a cenotaph.

These earthworks are scattered over the entire British landscape, and they can also be found in many parts of Europe and the rest of the world. Due to the prominence of barrows, archaeologists have categorized them into a number of types, often based on their location, form or date of construction. Some of the more common types include long barrows, round barrows, ring barrows, oval barrows and bank barrows.

Generally, the earliest form of barrow was the earthen (built without stone) long barrow, some of which have been dated from the 4th millennium BC. Typically, these were later followed by long barrows with internal chambers constructed from stone. West Kennet Long Barrow is an archetypal example of a long barrow, with excavations showing an internal stone structure divided into a number of 'rooms' and containing at least forty-six burials. Finally, later in the early Bronze Age, the round barrow became more popular, often in the shape of a bell or disc. These chronological shifts are generalized, as there are cases of barrows being reused in phases often separated by long periods. This is the case at the Barrow Clump site, which provides a continual

RIGHT: *West Kennet Long Barrow from the air.*

ABOVE: *Service personnel from Operation Nightingale working in Phil's trench.*

attention to antiquarian pursuits in 1804 and subsequently published a copy of Cunnington's site reports and drawings in a book entitled *The Ancient History of Wiltshire* in 1810.

The methods of Cunnington and his team were undoubtedly crude, and the digs were predominantly focused on uncovering hidden ancient treasure for antiquarian collections, rather than understanding the barrows and the lives of those who constructed them. However, it is important to remember that no previous archaeological guidelines or experience existed. Archaeologists of this period would often dig a central vertical shaft into the selected barrow in order to reveal its central contents, before gangs of unskilled labourers would excavate a trench (or cutting, as Hoare referred to it) through the barrow, to the centre and often out the other side. In spite of these techniques, Cunnington did make meticulous recordings, plans and drawings of the mainly Neolithic and Bronze Age barrows, and some of the terms he coined to describe the feature are still in use today. These early excavations were important steps towards the development of an archaeological discipline, including the first reference to the use of a trowel on an archaeological site, in a letter from Cunnington to Hoare in 1808.

Today, barrows are excavated, surveyed and recorded with painstaking precision. This is in part due to huge advancements in archaeological techniques, but also because the majority of surviving barrows are listed as Scheduled Ancient Monuments, and so they need to be excavated in a way that reflects their national importance. The Barrow Clump site is being excavated in a number of sections across the barrow. Each digging season focuses on a particular section or two. Digging the site in this manner allows for the entire area to be fully excavated in a couple of years, so that the archaeological remains are preserved and the badgers get their set back.

story from the Neolithic until the Anglo-Saxon period (4000 BC–AD 1066), making it significant in terms of both local and national heritage.

Not only do barrows provide archaeologists with a wonderful insight into the lives and burial practices of prehistoric societies, they were also integral to the development of archaeology as an academic discipline. The earliest recorded barrow digs occurred in 1237, when Henry III granted permission for his brother, the Earl of Cornwall, to dig a number of Cornish barrows. However, barrow digging reached its peak in the early nineteenth century, when one of the first modern archaeologists, William Cunnington, along with his regular excavators, Stephen and John Parker of Heytesbury, proceeded to dig 465 barrows in Wiltshire during a fifteen-year period (1803–18). The work was largely funded by Sir Richard Colt Hoare, an extremely wealthy man who turned his

HOW TO EXCAVATE A SKELETON

Contextual information

One of the things that surprised me about the site at Barrow Clump is just how many skeletons there were. The graves were so densely packed that more than one family and more than one generation must have been buried there. We still haven't got a complete handle on the timescale, because a lot of the finds are not terrifically diagnostic in terms of dating and phasing. However, the skeletons that have been found so far show a range of ages – we have children, babies and adults, both females and males – so it was obviously a domestic cemetery.

 It's fairly typical for the Anglo-Saxons to have had their cemeteries overlooking water courses, as is the case at Barrow Clump with the River Avon laying down in the valley below. Given its location, the cemetery would have been highly visible to nearby settlements, and I think they would have chosen this spot because it was a very prominent place in the landscape.

Bone preservation

There are three major problems regarding bone preservation on this site. The first is to do with the surrounding natural chalk – the underlying geology. Although chalk is alkaline and so doesn't tend to attack the mineral component (around 70 per cent) in the bone, graves cut into the chalk have a relatively solid base, which would hold the fluids from the decomposing body for longer than, say, a grave cut into a soil matrix. Those fluids would create a more acidic environment, predominantly around the central area of the body (the trunk), accelerating bone decomposition, particularly of the spongy bones comprising the spine and pelvis. Then there are the badgers, which have caused large amounts of damage. In one case, there are two badger runs cutting straight through a grave, totally removing the foot bones. The last problem is the trees: these are part of a late-eighteenth-century plantation, and the roots have happily made a home in the graves, working their way through and around the bones with obvious repercussions.

RIGHT: *Jackie pointing out where a badger run has gone across the grave, taking out part of the skeleton's hands. Note the spearhead just below the skull.*

ABOVE: *Jackie McKinley excavating around the hand of a skeleton using the famous family heirloom spoon.*

Tools

One of the key tools I use when excavating a skeleton is a spoon. I have a very pliable nickel-silver spoon I 'acquired' from my mum, which, combined with a half-inch paintbrush, is very handy for removing soil from confined spaces where a shovel will not fit – like around the ribs. In the image opposite you can see that I'm cleaning up the area around the hand bones, some of which are very small and can easily be missed. In order to be sure we recover all the bones, we collect all the soil around certain parts of the skeleton – in this case each hand – and put it in individually labelled sample bags, which will then be wet sieved and sorted back in the office.

Most memorable skeleton on *Time Team*

I always find the human skeleton fascinating: we all have one inside of us, and it reflects so much about an individual, especially when you see how it adapts to the pressures put on it. However, I have to say the most memorable skeleton for me was one we found when we were on the Isle of Man. Here the graves were stone-lined cists with very little soil in them. I still remember to this day when we lifted the cap stone off the grave and there was a plait of hair lying over the right shoulder of the female skeleton inside. That was just so startling and so personal – that the woman's hair had been preserved, and that when she had been placed into the grave the people burying her had so carefully arranged it.

Jackie McKinley

The process of excavating a burial is something that Jackie has been involved in for most of her archaeological life. In the mini skills masterclass on page 74 she explains some of the key aspects of this essential archaeological skill.

In Phil's trench a large amount of topsoil had been removed by mid-afternoon on Day One, but as yet there was little sign of any burials. For whatever reason, there seemed to have been less activity in this part of the site, although we were still only in the top half-metre or so. Working alongside Phil was Dave, who had been so badly injured in Afghanistan that he nearly died three times on the operating table. We were able to listen to his harrowing story.

One day in 2004 I was involved with regular convoy duties escorting a bomb-disposal team when I was caught up in a suicide car-bomb attack. I was blown into a nearby field and later found wandering and still on fire by locals. To this day, my memory of the event is hazy. I suffered multiple injuries, including the near-amputation of an arm.

I have very strong memories of the way that Dave was able to get himself into difficult positions during the excavation, in spite of the damage he had suffered to his arms. His contribution to the work we did in this important trench would turn out to be critical.

With all the trenches progressing well, it gave us a chance to review the general historical background of the site. The Anglo-Saxons were a combination of tribes from north-western Europe. The three key tribes were Angles, Saxons and Jutes. As Helen pointed out, these were people who had Germanic roots, so she questions the tendency to refer to them as 'Anglo'. We know their cultural background through their dress and writing: it's clear that they were sophisticated people, trading regularly with the Baltic and Middle East.

RIGHT: *Jackie discussing strategy with Sergeant Diarmaid Walshe and Tony on Day Three. Jackie was the lead archaeologist on this site for* Time Team.

The number of weapons in the cemetery suggests a community in which warriors played a key role; exactly how active they were is always the subject of much archaeological discussion and uncertainty. It seems that there were battles for territory going on in the fifth century, and there is a reference to a battle against the indigenous Britons at Old Sarum near Salisbury in AD 552; but there were also people who were settling down with their families and beginning to live in peace. One interesting question that needed to be answered would be the location of the settlement that these people came from.

Towards the end of Day One, Jackie discovered a fascinating bone fragment that could be evidence of more warlike activity. This was the arm bone of a woman that had a classic parry fracture in it: where the arm is thrown up to defend the head or face and the bone is broken by a downward blow.

In Cassie and Rob's trench, we were beginning to find evidence of a shield boss – the metal

ABOVE: *A shield boss from one of the burials. Note the fineness of the tool used to excavate at this stage.*

centre of a wooden shield. A shield is chiefly defensive but could also be used as an offensive weapon. Shields are a relatively common find in Anglo-Saxon cemeteries. In the *Time Team* live programme on Bawsey, shown in 1999, we reconstructed an Anglo-Saxon burial using some re-enactors, and it was interesting to see how placing the shield over the body and the face covered the person when the grave was refilled.

One of the most interesting parts of the project was the decision to get our diggers to live alongside the soldiers in the tented camps set up next to the site. This doubtless allowed them to immerse themselves in the project and the team spirit, but also had the added advantage of them not having to walk too far for some food and a pint at the end of the day. For the soldiers and *Time Team* diggers, Day One ended with a barbecue and some liquid refreshment.

Bones from one of the burials, showing a mended 'parry' fracture.

ANGLO-SAXON POTTERY

The end of the Roman occupation of Britain in the early fifth century saw a collapse in the industrialized manufacture of pottery. The people of Anglo-Saxon England went back to making pots using methods from the Iron Age, building them up by hand and firing them in bonfires, with most of them being made by the people who were going to use them, rather than professional potters.

The typical pottery of the early Anglo-Saxon period is the hand-built jar. Usually of simple shapes and without decoration, these jars were used for a variety of everyday tasks, particularly cooking. The mixture of inclusions in the clay varies enormously across the country, as people usually dug the clay around or near where they lived. For example, in Leicestershire granite-tempered pottery is the most common, whereas in East Anglia much of the pottery is sand-tempered, reflecting the composition of the local clays.

Undecorated Anglo-Saxon pottery is very difficult to date, as the shapes did not change much over time, other than a few distinctive forms. Decorated wares, although rarer, can be dated more closely. Certainly decorated pottery was far more common as grave goods or cremation containers: around a quarter of the pottery used for these purposes was decorated, while as much as 95 per cent of the pottery from settlement sites was plain. The Anglo-Saxon cemetery at South Carlton produced its own pots, including an urned cremation, but they were all plain.

With the arrival of Christianity, Anglo-Saxon trade with continental Europe increased dramatically, most of it connected to religious houses and royalty. One of the most sought-after commodities was wine, which had very high status in England at the time. We see evidence of wine arriving from the seventh century onwards in ports such as London, Ipswich and Southampton, in the form of wine barrels from the Rhineland and pottery from France and Germany. During the eighth century, pottery wine vessels began to arrive in the country in increasing quantities, and although it is mainly found at coastal ports and trading sites, such as the sherd discovered at St Osyth, it is very rare inland. When examples are found inland, it is usually at royal sites or monasteries, probably the only places that could afford an imported luxury such as wine at that time.

During the eighth and ninth centuries, most of the pottery made in England continued to be simple hand-built jar forms made from local clays and fired in bonfires, even in large ports such as London, York and Southampton. Despite the fact that imported wheel-made pottery was common in the ports, no attempts were made to copy it.

ABOVE: *A piece of Anglo-Saxon pot, showing the curved rim and stamped decoration.*

ABOVE: *Anglo-Saxon grass-tempered ware. The dark marks are the remnants of burnt-out organic material.*

The exception was Ipswich, where in around AD 720 potters in the town began to make pots on turntables and fire them in kilns for the first time since the Romans left. Frisian merchants were very active around the North Sea at the time, so it is thought that they may have brought the technology to Ipswich; alternatively Frisians may have lived in the area in such numbers that local potters began to make pottery based on Frisian types as there was a market for it. Soon the whole of East Anglia was using pots of this kind, and sherds have been found as far north as Yorkshire and as far west as Gloucestershire. It was probably being traded over such long distances as jugs became fashionable, and the jars were being used as containers for salt, a very important commodity at that time.

The late Saxon period saw a dramatic change in pottery-making in England, with fully wheel-thrown pottery fired in kilns being made in the new towns of the Midlands and East Anglia. Stamford ware was probably the first of the new wheel-thrown pottery types to be made. The earliest-known kiln dates to around AD 850, but as pottery of the same type was found in earlier deposits, it could have been made as early as AD 800. Like Ipswich ware, it is very different to other English pottery of the period, but very similar to continental wares, particularly pots made and used in northern France, Belgium and Holland. Stamford ware was very popular and is found all over Britain. It is also fairly common in the coastal ports of Ireland, although our understanding of it has recently been complicated by the discovery of a manufactory of virtually identical wares at Pontefract in Yorkshire. There seems little doubt that the first Stamford-ware potters came from France, as the pottery and technology used for making it is so similar.

At around the same time that Stamford ware was first being manufactured, potters began to make similar pottery in Ipswich. Over the next hundred years, many of the other towns in the Midlands and East Anglia began to follow suit, including Thetford. Such pottery is, like Stamford ware, wheel-thrown and kiln-fired, but is usually grey in colour and never glazed. The Thetford industry, despite not starting until around the beginning of the tenth century, was the first to be recognized by archaeologists, and so Thetford ware is the general name given to such pottery, with kilns known to have existed in Norwich and Ipswich, as well as in rural areas such as Langhale in Norfolk. Thetford ware was mass produced in vast quantities. Like Stamford ware, the original technology is thought to have come from France, as the material and the kilns are very similar to grey wares made and used in north France and Belgium.

See pages 92–3 for more examples of Anglo-Saxon pottery.

Paul Blinkhorn

Day Two started with one of the less welcoming aspects of army life: a bugle call to get the diggers out of bed.

JACKIE WAS WORKING on one of the main skeletons and was able to confirm from the wide sciatic notch that it was a female (see mini skills masterclass on page 84). The skeleton had been heavily 'badgered', as she put it. The grave cut itself had been dug into the ditch of the Bronze Age barrow, and she was able to see the small scratch marks where the chalk bank had been widened to accommodate the feet of the burial. In Trench 1 Phil was still finding little evidence of burials, but he was considerably cheered up by the appearance of pieces of Neolithic flint.

In Cassie's trench the shield boss continued to be cleaned. One of the soldiers was able to describe the amazing sixth-century drinking vessel that had been found near their burial, made from yew with hoops and strips of metal reinforcement. We were able to see this being X-rayed on a portable machine that had recently been in service in Afghanistan X-raying injured soldiers. *Time Team* has excavated Anglo-Saxon drinking vessels before, in Bremmer. Later in the day this same X-ray machine would reveal a diamond-shaped mount on our shield boss, which, as Helen pointed out, showed that the shields had both a military and a decorative function.

Raksha was excavating in a trench near to what may have been the centre of the barrow. Some of the finds seemed to indicate the presence of cremations in this area. Trench 1 had shown that this area of the mound contained very few burials, but it was producing sherds of

ABOVE: *Jackie excavating around the pelvis of a burial. This is potentially an important area where small finds can appear.*

ABOVE: *A shield boss from the centre of an Anglo-Saxon shield, one of our key finds.*

Bronze Age pottery and evidence of a ditch that was part of the Bronze Age burial mound. The pottery dating from 2,200 BC was similar to that found in association with the main site at Stonehenge.

At the end of Day Two, I began to feel that although the trench that had occupied Phil for two days had begun to deliver, it was important to put him into another key element of the site, which would hopefully involve him working on an Anglo-Saxon burial. This strategic moving of Phil was outside of the parameters of the original script and was met with a degree of reluctance from some of the production team. It was another example of the archaeological reality being in conflict with our production schedule. From the viewers' perspective, I always want Phil to be at the centre of the action. I discussed the matter with Diarmaid and asked him if there were any specific areas where we could use Phil usefully on the final day.

In the far corner of the mound, one particular trench with very clear badger tunnels cutting through it had revealed what was possibly another Anglo-Saxon burial in the section of a previous trench. To ask for this to be excavated in the time that we had left was, as I was only too aware, quite a challenge, but Diarmaid was willing to listen to our proposals. As the day came to an end, with the support of Phil Andrews, the Wessex supervisor, it seemed like it might be possible to go ahead. Diarmaid's final words to me were: 'I need to talk to Richard, and if he agrees then it's a goer.' During the previous two days we had received a lot of support from Richard Osgood; as the chief MoD archaeologist, I felt that he would recognize the value of getting Phil involved, both from an archaeological point of view and from the way this would enhance the final day's film coverage.

RESCUE ARCHAEOLOGY

Rescue archaeology (also known as salvage archaeology, commercial archaeology or preventative archaeology) is the practice of conducting archaeological techniques such as survey and excavation in areas threatened by natural events, construction or other land developments. In the case of Barrow Clump, badgers had built a large and continually

ABOVE: *These holes are typical of the kind of damage wreaked by badgers on an archaeological site.*

expanding set through the majority of the remains, causing the site to be placed on the English Heritage at Risk Register. The work conducted by Operation Nightingale was an essential form of rescue archaeology, the objective being to learn and record as much as possible about the remaining deposits before the entire site succumbed to the actions of the badgers. This work was not only in the interest of archaeologists but also the badgers, as once the site has been fully excavated, it can be returned to the badgers for their uninterrupted use.

The rescue archaeology occurring at Barrow Clump is a direct result of natural processes affecting the site. However, the majority of rescue archaeology projects tend to occur in urban areas undergoing redevelopment or brand-new construction sites. Originally archaeologists relied on the goodwill of developers to provide them with the opportunity to record remains, but since 1990 it has been a legal requirement that archaeological survey must be permitted prior to the development or construction of a site. As a result of this, various organizations providing contract archaeological services have sprung up around the country: in 2010 over 3,000 archaeologists were employed within these commercial archaeological units.

The ever-increasing threat of coastal erosion and climate change means that more and more sites are now in need of rescue archaeology techniques. A good example of this would be *Time Team*'s work on the prehistoric monument of Seahenge in Norfolk, where the archaeology had to be conducted at great speed in order to preserve the remains before they were destroyed by the sea. Although this monument was saved, there are still many prehistoric monuments within the area that remain under threat.

It was with some trepidation that at 8.30 a.m. I sought out Diarmaid to find out the final decision about the extra trench.

I WAS DELIGHTED to hear that Richard had given his approval and that they would organize some of the Operation Nightingale team to help remove the topsoil and the overburden that was covering the skeleton. The question in my mind was: would it be worth it? All that we could see was a slender arm bone of an Anglo-Saxon burial appearing out of the section; given the degree of badger activity in the area, we would be lucky to find anything else.

The atmosphere on the site on the final day was incredibly encouraging. We all got a sense of how focused the soldiers were and how working in a team on an important project that required precision, care and skill provided an ideal focus for those involved. A soldier, when given orders, has to intelligently carry them out. As I looked around the site at about 10 a.m. on the final day,

all I could see were teams of archaeologists, soldiers and other volunteers working with complete concentration on the task in hand. Any sense of the injuries they carried, both physical and emotional, had become completely secondary to the task in hand. A lot of the hard work in Phil's trench was being done by soldiers with what appeared to be major damage to their legs and arms, but none of them gave this a second thought as they applied themselves 100 per cent to the task in hand.

Phil's enthusiasm for this project had been clear from the start. Halfway through the morning, I began to hear noises from the trench that were the unmistakable sounds of a happy Harding with fantastic archaeology appearing at the end of his trowel.

The burial in Phil's trench appeared to be relatively intact: there was enough of the skeleton to suggest that if there were grave goods, these might be recoverable in the time we had left. Phil's skeleton was gradually revealing its secrets. According to Jackie, it was a small female burial, and considering the chaos caused by badger tunnels all around it, it had survived remarkably well. As we watched Phil's gentle excavation of the area around the skull, small glass beads began to appear, which Helen believed to be Roman in origin, and on either side of the skull was a small square-headed brooch, which Helen described as sensational. To watch as Phil and his team excavated what I had begun to think of as an Anglo-Saxon princess was one of the most exciting moments of our year.

LEFT: *Phil and service personnel examining the details of a trench.*

HOW TO INTERPRET A SKELETON

Sexing

The first port of call when sexing a skeleton is the pelvis: because females are designed to have babies and males aren't, you get slight variations in the shape (morphology) of the pelvic bones, creating more space for the developing foetus. This doesn't mean to say the female's bones are bigger – generally the male pelvic bones will be larger – but there are variations in the sharpness of angles in the bones and the way the area is opened up in the female. For example, in males, the greater sciatic notch (behind the hip joint to either side of where the pelvis articulates with the base of the spine) tends to be tight, forming an acute V-shape, while in the female the angle is wider, forming more of a broad U-shape, which opens up the pelvic girdle.

The skull also reveals a lot of information about the sex of an individual. Basically, male skulls are generally bigger and lumpier than female skulls. For example, the margins of the eye sockets are fairly sharp in the female and

ABOVE: *The pelvic area of a burial, showing the sciatic notch.*

tend to be broader and more rounded in the male, and males often develop strong supra-orbital ridges – think of Neanderthal brow ridges, but scaled down a bit! Another key area is at the back of the skull, where the big neck muscles are attached, which is called the nuchal crest or external occipital protuberance. Males tend to develop a strong nuchal crest, either as a marked ridge or sometimes as what looks like a 'tongue' of bone, whereas in females it's less pronounced or almost non-existent.

Ageing a skeleton

Teeth can reveal a great deal of information about an individual, including helping to estimate a person's age and giving clues as to their diet and level of oral hygiene. Tooth development is the most reliable way of ageing children and teenagers. For example, this skeleton at Barrow Clump is that of an immature individual: you can clearly see the erupted permanent teeth alongside the developing crown of the third molar (or 'wisdom tooth'), which is still in the crown crypt.

Tooth wear patterns are used to help age adults. Bone, being a combination of mineral and organic tissues, will regenerate over time, but tooth enamel is only mineral; although it's very

ABOVE: *Jackie and Phil excavating a grave at Westminster Abbey.*

tough, once it's worn away it does not regenerate. Consequently, teeth get increasingly worn down as an adult ages.

The other main method used to age a skeleton is bone fusion. Most individual bones develop from several centres of ossification, allowing for growth. Most long bones (the major limb bones) develop with three or more centres, one for the shaft of the bone (diaphysis) and one or more at each of the growing ends, forming the joints (epiphyses). These develop with age and the various epiphyses eventually fuse together. So when we are trying to ascertain the age of a youngster, we will look both at the length of the long bones (which can be slightly variable dependent on diet and general health) and at the stage of epiphyseal fusion. Using this information and that from the teeth, individuals can be aged quite closely up to about eighteen, when most of the bones will be fused and the person will have finished growing – at least upwards! The last epiphyseal fusion takes place around twenty-five to twenty-eight years of age, in the collar bone, where it articulates with the upper part of the breast bone.

Palaeopathology

This is the study of ancient diseases. The osteoarchaeologist looks for evidence of chronic conditions that people suffered from, rather than what they died of, because it generally takes time for bone to react to disease. Diseases such as leprosy can cause changes in the skeleton: bone is destroyed, so that eventually the teeth fall out (no sockets for them to sit in) and the nose disappears, causing the face to appear 'collapsed'. However, a person could suffer from leprosy for years before any signs of it appear in the skeleton. Syphilis also has quite horrendous effects on skeletons over time, causing a lot of bone destruction, with destructive lesions on the skull and ulcerations in the legs.

ABOVE: *A teenager's mandible (lower jaw), showing the erupted permanent teeth with the unerupted and still-forming third molar in the crown crypt (lower left).*

Diet

The patterns of dental disease can tell us a lot about what people ate, while the analysis of carbon and nitrogen isotopes in the bone can illustrate people's dietary preferences. At a very basic level, this can help us to determine an individual's position in the food chain, demonstrating differences between vegetarians and meat-eaters (the latter are higher up the chain), or, most interestingly, between marine and terrestrial foodstuffs. This not only helps us to understand how humans exploited their environment, but also has economic and social implications.

Jackie McKinley

ABOVE: *Jackie carefully surveying and drawing the grave cut and skeleton.*

ABOVE: *Looking into the face of an Anglo-Saxon burial. The chalk packed around the skull may have helped to preserve the bone by creating a non-acidic environment.*

Helen was genuinely flabbergasted by the minute scale of the jewellery found in this burial. She described the beads as 'doll's-house jewellery'. By covering their excavation in detail, we were able to record one of the great moments of *Time Team*. Helen was particularly excited by the workmanship on the brooch. Subsequent excavation of this burial by Diarmaid and his team would reveal more beads, a knife and other grave goods. It created a fitting climax for one of the best *Time Team* digs ever.

One of the breakthroughs on Day Three was made by Emma, who was analysing the topographic evidence from the LiDAR survey, using what she called 'view shed analysis'. This enabled us to analyse the landscape in a way that shows what can be seen from various places. The prominence of the barrow would have been

ABOVE RIGHT: *This small square-headed brooch was one of our best finds. Helen was amazed by the small size – it was, only around 4 centimetres (1½ in) in length.*

Small Anglo-Saxon bead, found with the skeleton in Phil's final trench at Barrow Clump.

important to the Anglo-Saxon community; in general, we believe that Anglo-Saxon villages have a topographic relationship with the burial sites of their dead.

Emma was able to show that Barrow Clump can be seen from Figeldean, and this fact may have played an important role in the life of the community. It may also explain why the area of the mound uncovered in Phil's long trench was less used, being the part of the hill that was least visible from the settlement. Helen also made the observation that the early burials on the site seemed to have been concentrated in the original Bronze Age ditch area. By analysing an X-ray of a spearhead, she was able to show that its particular typology, which included a blade with a carved back, implied a later date, and this may mean that the burials nearer the centre of the mound were part of a later phase of use once the earlier sites had been occupied.

When I looked around at the site on Day Three and saw the way the team was working, it made me feel that here was a group of archaeologists you would want to take with you anywhere in the world to dig on important sites. For all of us, the facts of their different disabilities had faded into the background. They were just a group of people who loved archaeology as much as us, and their dedication and focus on the work, despite the challenges they faced, created an impressive example for everyone. The Operation Nightingale team will be returning to the Barrow Clump site next year, and I hope we will be able to join them.

ANGLO-SAXON JEWELLERY

The Anglo-Saxon people were known for their beautiful jewellery, in particular a wide variety of often elaborate and delicate brooches. These brooches are typically found as part of an assemblage of female grave goods, like the brooch discovered by Operation Nightingale and *Time Team* at the Barrow Clump site. Known by the Anglo-Saxons as dalc or spennels, brooches seem to have been commonly worn in pairs, with one on each collar bone, presumably to fasten the peplo – a tubular-style dress. Examples of brooches found on the Continent typically appear as matching pairs, while those from England (particularly those from the early Anglo-Saxon period) are commonly mismatched. Between the two brooches a connecting chain was often worn across the chest. The chains are rarely found in an archaeological context, with only one or two having been discovered within the Salisbury area. This may in part be due to the delicateness of their design, which made them unlikely to survive deposition, or because their pure metal content made them worth recycling.

The key point to bear in mind when examining Anglo-Saxon brooches is that their primary function was decorative. Though the artefacts have a clear practical purpose in securing clothing, they were used to display a range of information including rank, wealth and ethnicity through their shape, style, material and decoration, rendering their principal purpose symbolic.

A huge variety of shapes exists, from cruciforms and discs to brooches shaped to look like animals. The brooch found in Phil's trench on the last day of *Time Team*'s visit to the Barrow Clump site was of the square-headed variety, a type largely seen in England around the end of the fifth century. A square-headed brooch is a very rare find, particularly those as small as the one at Barrow Clump. The rareness of these finds suggests they may have been worn by the most prominent families within rural groups.

The huge variety in styles of brooches found has allowed archaeologists to build a detailed finds database. Generally, it seems that specific female brooch designs tend to be localised to specific areas. On the rare occasions when particular styles of brooch are found 'out of place'

ABOVE: *A beautiful square-headed Anglo-Saxon brooch uncovered at an earlier* Time Team *excavation.*

ABOVE: *A square-headed Anglo-Saxon brooch, dating to the early sixth century. This came from an earlier English Heritage excavation at Barrow Clump.*

it may be because the women in question had migrated away from their birthplace, most likely through marriage into a different village. Interestingly, in the case of the square-headed brooch from the earlier years of the period, similar examples have been found in localized areas of both continental Europe and England. This evidence suggests that a variety of smaller differing cultural groups existed within the larger Anglo-Saxon group, who settled and populated distinct areas within England.

In addition to the style, the base metal of the brooch is believed to have identified individuals within a rigid hierarchy. At the top would have been those who wore brooches made from silver or gold, while those of the lowest rank would wear brooches made from brass with a very high zinc and tin content. Between these two extremes many of the brooches were made from bronze (copper alloy) or sometimes iron. These bronze brooches were often coated in silver or gold plate, sometimes just microns thick, in order to make them look more prestigious.

Brooch decoration was also hugely important, and again a wide variety of decoration exists, from the very plain to extremely intricate. Many brooches have been found that are decorated with augmented enamelling, cloisonné work or sometimes even millefiori: a series of thin stretched glass rods, which are then heated, spun and stretched so that the colours mingle, creating a symmetrical pattern within a circle. Decoration of this kind has led many archaeologists to theorize that light was incredibly important to Anglo-Saxons. From the design of church windows to the decoration on brooches, effects were carefully crafted in order to specifically catch and reflect the light.

Studying these intriguing artefacts also helps shine a light on the people who made them. The archaeological database suggests that individual brooch-makers would have travelled across the countryside with portable foundries or smelting kits and a series of moulds shaped to produce standard brooches. In recent years a number of founders' hoards (buried assemblages of scrap metal) have been excavated. One suggestion as to the dynamics of the brooch trade is that if a brooch broke, the owner would have kept it until the next time a portable foundry visited the village. The brooch could then be fixed and paid for in leftover scrap metal. According to this interpretation, the cumulative weight of scrap metal may have forced the individuals working these portable foundries to bury some of their stash, with the intention of returning to collect it at a later time.

RIGHT: *Saxon disc brooch, also sixth-century. This was discovered by Operation Nightingale after the* Time Team *shoot, in the grave Phil had been excavating.*

VIEW FROM THE TRENCHES

ROB

The quality of the archaeology, the buzz on site, the hospitality and the professionalism of Operation Nightingale all contributed to an unforgettable experience at Barrow Clump. Diggers have a reputation for being hard-bitten and cynical, but for me this was one of those occasions that make you thank your lucky stars that you're an archaeologist.

Ordinarily, *Time Team* arrive to be presented with a blank canvas, but in this case the excavation was already in full swing, with two 'slices' of the barrow stripped back to the chalk and teams of soldiers and students meticulously exposing what seemed like a never-ending series of spectacular Saxon burials.

I began by cleaning out the remnants of long-disused badger sets within the barrow mound itself, removing the loose infill of the tunnel and sifting the loose spoil for stray finds: burrowing animals are notorious for their ability to move bones and artefacts surprisingly long distances! The extent of the badger disturbance was immediately obvious, and highlighted the necessity of excavating the site before its unique secrets are lost.

Day Two saw me turn my attention to the long trench we had opened on the north side of the barrow, running from the apex to beyond the projected extent of the outer ditch. Prior

ABOVE: *Service personnel from Operation Nightingale working on surveys of a trench.*

work on the site had identified an earlier circular ditch underlying the mound (usually composed of the material dug out from the outer ditch and topped with a chalk 'cap' to give a gleaming white finish). A thorough clean was going to be necessary if we were going to be able to unpick the relationships between the earlier ditch, the mound and the outer ditch. We were working from the 'known' point, around the apex of the barrow, to the 'unknown' sequence of deposits stretching down towards the outer ditch. Working 'from the known to the unknown' is a mantra oft-repeated by diggers, instilled in me on my first excavation as a professional archaeologist by none other than *Time Team*'s own Tracey Smith!

It wasn't long before we were down to fragmentary, compacted chalk – seemingly the remnants of the mound. But then, as we worked back towards the ditch, we came to the edge of the redeposited chalk and onto a darker deposit of fine, sandier soil. As we were cleaning back, a piece of worked flint appeared. It was unmistakably a piece of knapping debitage: the waste flakes produced during the manufacture of stone tools. Careful sieving of the spoil as we proceeded yielded a tray full of pieces. While the discovery of piles of discarded waste might not seem as glamorous as a finely worked arrowhead, for those of us who love prehistory it tells a story. Knappers didn't usually move piles of debitage – it had no useful function, so it tended to be left where it fell – so these finds indicated that people were knapping on this very spot.

The presence of the flint posed an intriguing question. The deposit within which it lay appeared to run underneath the chalky deposit, thus predating the mound. The flint scatter evidently belonged either to an earlier phase of activity, possibly linked to the ring ditch lying beneath the mound, or to the construction phase of the barrow.

On the morning of Day Three, I took over the outer ditch slot from Phil, to find out whether Saxon burials, so dense around the south of the barrow, were present on the north side. Balancing the need to be constantly alert for human remains, particularly given the near-invisibility of some of the grave cuts elsewhere on the site, with the need to excavate efficiently demanded stamina, skill, quick wits and stoicism. My team possessed these qualities in spades, doing a thorough job and demonstrating a grasp of the key archaeological issues that would put

ABOVE: *Rob watching the service personnel at work at Barrow Clump.*

some professionals to shame. By the end of the day we'd bottomed and cleaned out the ditch.

We didn't encounter any Saxon graves within the ditch, raising the intriguing possibility that the later cemetery was intentionally restricted to one part of the barrow. Why? It's difficult to say: as so often in archaeology, answering one question has thrown up a whole lot more!

ANGLO-SAXON POTTERY: 5TH CENTURY AD–1066

Some typical examples and how to identify them

1. Hand-built pottery

The classic early Anglo-Saxon pottery type, known variously as grass-tempered, chaff-tempered or organic-tempered ware, has a very light and fairly soft 'corky' fabric due to the clay being mixed with organic material, probably in the form of animal dung. The potters would often wipe the surface of these pots with wet hands to cover the inclusions, but when a sherd is viewed in section it is possible to see the characteristic seed- and grass-shaped voids where the organic material was burnt out during firing.

2. Decorated hand-built pottery

During the fifth century, most pottery was decorated with simple patterns of incised lines and dots, with bosses becoming more common at the end of the fifth century. This period also saw the general uptake of stamped decoration, and by the middle of the sixth century most pots were decorated only with stamps and incised lines, with the stamps often arranged as pendant triangles. By the middle of the seventh century, pots became entirely plain, possibly because decorated pottery was closely associated with pagan burial.

3. Ipswich ware

Ipswich ware is very different to the Anglo-Saxon pottery that preceded it, being hard and usually grey in colour, with quite thick-walled and clumsy vessels. Most of the pots were jars, but the Ipswich potters also made jugs – again, the first time such pottery had been made since Roman times. Ipswich-ware jugs were decorated with stamping, and some of the decorative arrangements, particularly pendant triangles, were similar to those used in pagan times. Ipswich-ware jugs are very different in shape to the imported French and German jugs of the period, and the jars are different to other English types, but both jugs and jars are very similar to those made by the Frisians of southern Holland.

4. Thetford ware

The vast majority of the pots made at Thetford were simple jars used for cooking and other everyday activities, but large storage jars were also made with applied strips, showing a passing similarity to relief-band amphorae. Lots of kilns have been discovered in Suffolk, and over a quarter of a million sherds have been excavated in Ipswich, despite the fact that only around 5 per cent of the Saxon town has been excavated.

OAKHAM CASTLE

Oakham was another of those *Time Team* sites that made us realize how many fascinating places are tucked away in the British countryside waiting to be discovered.

THIS HAS BEEN one of the joys of working on *Time Team*. Very few of us were aware of the existence of the massive Norman hall at the centre of the site, the best-preserved example of its kind in the country.

Rutland is also an area that came as a complete surprise. Full of fascinating small villages, the county has an ancient history of being almost a kingdom in its own right. Rutland maintained its independence for many years and was the last area of Britain to come under the control of the crown. The Great Hall at the castle is decorated with a unique collection of oversized horseshoes: these were given to the county as a symbol of its independence by a succession of noblemen. Peers of the realm were expected to give a large decorative horseshoe when they visited, a tradition that began in the time of Walkelin de Ferrers, a Norman baron. The name Ferrers actually means farrier or blacksmith.

I am always interested when we have colourful characters connected with the site, and at Oakham we had two: Walkelin de Ferrers, a close friend of Richard the Lionheart, and the Saxon Queen Edith, wife of Edward the Confessor.

In contrast to the wonderfully preserved Great Hall, the rest of the site was occupied by an area of 'lumps and bumps', as Stewart likes to call

them: earthworks which betrayed the presence of buildings and other structures, but about which surprisingly little was known. Would they turn out to be contemporary with the hall itself?

This site would present us with an unusual challenge. Early on Day One it became apparent that the geophysics was having trouble with the

RIGHT: *Richard K. Morris examining the columns in the Great Hall at Oakham. Richard would help us decipher the architectural remains of the Great Hall.*

soil conditions and unable to produce the clear results we usually expect. This meant that we would have to rely on two different skills to help us locate the trenches: Stewart's ability to record and decipher earthworks; and Richard K. Morris's skill at interpreting standing buildings. This would be a *Time Team* that, for the most part, would not be able to rely on geophysics.

Because the site was a Scheduled Ancient Monument, this programme would illustrate an important aspect of our archaeological work: the relationship with English Heritage. We would be working closely with an English Heritage inspector, Tim Allen, and this also meant that Jim Mower, the development producer, was under extra pressure to develop a project design that would be acceptable to English Heritage.

Oakham also gave Stewart a chance to undertake an analysis of the relationship between the hall and the town itself. As the programme progressed, he would take the town plan of Oakham back from the present day to its Saxon origins.

On Day One we found a huge contrast between the main standing building, Britain's best-preserved Norman hall, and the earthworks that surrounded it. As is often the case, a lot was known about the main structure, but we had been asked by English Heritage to explore the area outside, between the hall and the defensive wall that enclosed it. As this was an English Heritage site, we would be limited as to the number of trenches and the area we could dig. One of the important things we do is to give English Heritage information that enables them to understand the condition of the remains they are looking after and how they can best be managed in the future.

BELOW: *A view of the beautifully preserved Great Hall.*

ABOVE: *Stewart was keen to set the Great Hall in the context of the town.*

A key element of the project design stressed the main goal of the work we would undertake. The project design for a *Time Team* excavation is set out as a series of research aims developed with the local archaeologists and, in the case of scheduled sites, English Heritage. The organization is a critical reference point for us during these excavations, and it is an important aspect of getting scheduled monument consent that we complete the research aims. The project design for Oakham included three main questions:

Research aim 1: What are the extent, condition, date range and function of surviving subsurface archaeological remains representing buildings associated with the twelfth-century hall within the inner bailey/ward at Oakham Castle? Previous geophysical surveys and minor archaeological interventions at Oakham Castle within the inner bailey/ward have identified good potential for well-preserved subsurface archaeological remains, likely to represent buildings associated with the standing twelfth-century hall.

Research aim 2: What are the extent, condition, date range and function of surviving subsurface archaeological remains predating the twelfth-century complex thought to have been constructed by Walkelin de Ferrers? Do these remains represent a royal Saxon burh, or fortified settlement? Documentary evidence and the results of previous interventions on site suggest that Oakham Castle may have been constructed within the core of a Saxon burh.

Research aim 3: Do the earthwork features comprising Cutts Close represent a relic of the Saxon burh, later truncated by twelfth-century construction? To what extent do late-Saxon deposits remain in situ? Previous interventions within Cutts Close have revealed evidence of mid- to late-Saxon activity on the site.

Oakham would also be a chance for us to work with Richard K. Morris, *Time Team*'s building expert: his crucial role would be to study the fabric of the hall for clues as to where we should look for other structures.

On Day One we set out the goals and as usual recorded Tony's opening piece to camera.

LEFT: *Trench 1 went in right against the wall of the main hall.*

TONY'S PIECE TO CAMERA

66 *Welcome to the village of Oakham. A place with a special secret and it's this: the best-preserved twelfth-century building in Britain. This site wasn't just home to Norman knights and lords: it once hosted some of the most legendary Saxon kings and queens in Britain. There's much more to Oakham Castle than meets the eye. Under these lumps and bumps lies some fascinating history.*

But we have a major challenge on our hands. I suspect there's a lot of archaeology concealed in this vast back garden here, and we have just three days to find out what's actually here and who built what – and who had to die before they could get their hands on it! 99

Oakham has been an important town since Saxon times. The wife of Edward the Confessor, Edith of Wessex, lived here until her death in 1075, which reflects the high status of this part of England at the time. As we all found out, it takes a long time to get here, travelling through many of Leicestershire's beautiful little villages, but in the past Oakham's remote location didn't prevent it from becoming a seat of power.

In the corner of the castle grounds are the remains of the original motte, or earthen mound, the earliest Norman structure. As part of the plan to exert Norman influence across the country after the conquest, numerous motte and bailey castles were created. Subsequently large stone structures were created around 1180–90 by Walkelin de Ferrers, including the Great Hall. Over its lifetime it has been used as a courtroom and for other legal purposes; this may have helped to preserve the structure from destruction.

A description of the castle written in 1340 described it as having 'a hall, four rooms, a

WHAT TO DO IF YOU FIND 'TREASURE'

The adage 'finders keepers' doesn't really apply in the world of archaeology. If you are lucky enough to find 'treasure', you are legally obliged to report it within fourteen days to either your district Finds Liaison Officer (see mini skills masterclass on page 50; visit www.finds.org to find out details of your nearest FLO), police station or local museum, who will then inform the relevant local coroner.

The penalty for not reporting a find that you believe to be potential treasure is up to three months in prison or a maximum fine of £5,000 under the 1996 Treasure Act, which applies in England, Wales and Northern Ireland. Scotland has its own, slightly different arrangements: for full details you should contact the Treasure Trove Unit of the National Museums of Scotland. Although the potential punishment may seem harsh, these laws are designed to ensure that finds of historic importance are properly recorded, rather than disappearing without trace into individual collections.

Succinctly defining what actually constitutes treasure is often complicated. The 1996 Treasure Act defines treasure as any find falling under one of the following categories:

- coins that are more than 300 years old at the time of discovery
- any metallic object more than 300 years old that contains at least 10 per cent gold/silver
- any group of two or more prehistoric metallic objects, no matter how small the metal content is
- any associated objects that are found in the same place as an item falling into one of the previous three categories.

ABOVE: *Using a metal detector to examine spoil on a* Time Team *site.*

In the case of coins, two or more silver or gold coins or ten or more copper alloy coins found together are considered a hoard and must be reported. Since 2002, the Treasure (Designation) Order broadened the definition to include two or more prehistoric base-metal assemblages, such as copper alloy artefacts. For instance, finding a Bronze Age axe and a Bronze Age chisel together would now qualify as treasure. The Treasure Act's Code of Practice, which can be easily accessed through the Department of Culture, Media and Sport's website, provides further information regarding the definition of treasure. However, if in doubt, the best advice is always to report the find and allow experts to decide if any of the criteria are met.

If experts decide your find is not classed as treasure, the Secretary of State will disclaim it and it may be returned to you without an inquest, depending on who owns the land. However, if the find is deemed to be treasure, your local Finds Liaison Officer will refer it on to the British Museum or the National Museums and Galleries of Wales. If no museum wishes to acquire the find, the object will be returned to the finder. If a museum does decide to purchase your find, a treasure valuation committee of independent antiques and coin experts will decide the likely market value of your find and, provided it was discovered legally, reimburse you for it.

As always, the golden rule is to take enormous care when handling any find. Never apply any substances to the find. If it is wet, keep it moist; or if this is not possible, let it dry very slowly. Always keep each find in a separate clearly labelled bag. Any attempts at cleaning or preserving, however well-intentioned, might easily harm or destroy the object. Additionally, it is always worth recording the exact location of where you discovered the find and how your discovery was made. Finally, in every case, seek expert advice as soon as possible.

ABOVE: *Two sides of a gold coin fron the reign of Henry V, one of* Time Team's *most memorable finds, discovered by a metal detectorist in the ditch at Codnor Castle, Derbyshire.*

ABOVE: *Ian Barclay opening a trench to look for structures surrounding the main hall.*

chapel, a kitchen, two stables, a barn for hay, a house for prisoners – the county gaol, a room for the gatekeeper and a drawbridge with iron chains'. I never particularly like these statements, as they make us hostages to fortune. A long description of what was there can look a bit embarrassing if we end up not being able to find anything in our excavations! All that remains of these elements today are a set of grass mounds, ridges and hollows.

While John began his geophysics survey, Stewart set about doing a landscape survey using the old-fashioned method of notebook and pencil. I asked him to describe how he actually

begins to look at the landscape in order to do this and exactly what all those little dots and squiggles mean; see the mini skills masterclass on page 108.

John's task was made difficult by the weather conditions, which had resulted in the soil becoming waterlogged. His two usual methods of 'mag' and 'res' (see mini skills masterclass on page 173) were unlikely to give useful results because the conditions would mean little contact between walls and soil – both being equally wet. John and Jimmy had to rely on radar. Once a grid had been put into place, they began the first scan. This gave Richard and Phil a chance to take a closer look at the Great Hall, to see if it would provide any clues as to where we should be looking for evidence of other buildings.

Examining a standing building – what Mick used to call vertical archaeology – is a real skill. It enables the archaeologist to unpick the structure and record the evidence that exists in small changes to the external structure. Remnants of previous walls can leave scars and other signs, and this might help us to work out where to look for these walls in the ground surrounding the main structure.

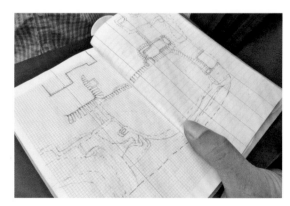

ABOVE: *Stewart's interpretations of the earthworks in his notebook.*

MINI SKILLS MASTERCLASS

LEFT: *Neil Holbrook and Phil looking at the exterior details of the hall.*

INTERPRETING A STANDING BUILDING

Building archaeologists deal with fabric, form and function: what a building is made of, how the materials were used, and what the building was for. To do our job thoroughly, we need to be observant, objective and open-minded – which often means throwing away the textbooks, even when dealing with a well-known building like Oakham Hall. The aisled interior is amazingly intact and the architectural detail of the arcades and windows are fairly easy to date to the late twelfth century.

Looking closely at the masonry also gives us an idea of which parts are original – such as the unusual horizontally striped sections – and where doorways or windows have been blocked or inserted. It is clear that the main south doorway, for example, has been moved to its present position from the east end of the south wall – a more conventional position.

What we really needed to know at Oakham was how this standing building related to others near to or even attached to it. There was no evidence that its walls continued in any direction – in fact the corners were neatly chamfered – and the windows in the side walls looked to be original. Any attached structures would have to have been added to the end walls, and be slightly narrower.

That hypothesis was supported by the archaeological evidence. The primary masonry of the end walls seemed slightly cruder. Meanwhile the plinths at the bottom of the side walls only continued for a short distance along them; surviving doorways did not seem to have been external ones, and there was no sign of any original windows. Even more significant was the odd but original setback, high up in the gable walls.

The evidence suggested that from the beginning there had been lower and slightly narrower structures attached to both ends of the Great Hall. The lack of scars on the masonry showed that these must have been of timber construction, and the unusual setback in the gables probably took the top timber of their lean-to roof structures. Being made of timber, their buried remnants would almost certainly be less substantial than the footings of their later stone-built replacements.

Richard K. Morris

ABOVE: *Matt checking out the potential trench site for underground cables, an important step before a trench is started.*

The first radar scans seemed to give us some clues, but they were not particularly clear. We also had drawings from a previous excavation to help us, and we were able to get Trench 1 in fairly early on the first day. A second trench was located over one of the ridges, as Stewart seemed to be convinced this represented the wall of a building. Tracey and Cassie would be in charge of this trench. It was an important test of our ability to evaluate one of the typical features that existed in the inner bailey around the Great Hall.

I asked Richard for an overview of the standing building remains and to tell me what he'd noticed.

It is clear that there has been a lot of change here at Oakham. What that was exactly we haven't worked out yet. The [Great] Hall is such an old building; it has been interfered with and altered many times. Take those strips up there: that is the remains of where the storage rooms would have been and what would have been the end of the hall where we are standing now. You are looking at hundreds of years' worth of use and alteration. The windows are medieval and the corridors led to what we have unearthed today. Some of the stonework and carving would date back as far as the Romans much earlier – around AD 80 – who were known to have drawn limestone from Clipsham quarry, a few miles away from here.

Standing in the central hall, Richard was able to give a detailed outline of the interior and history of Oakham. The Great Hall of Oakham Castle is one of the most important Norman buildings in England. While there are many fine Norman buildings surviving in the country, most of these are either defensive or religious. The Great Hall, despite being within a castle setting, is an extremely rare example of a twelfth-century domestic building and one that is surprisingly intact. Ironically, the defences within which it was situated are now fragmentary at best, and the rest of the buildings within the walls were demolished centuries ago.

The building is a stone-built aisled hall of four bays, roofed in Collyweston tile stones – the central 'nave' rising only slightly from the lean-to roofs of the aisles. The side walls have a plinth and were probably once decorated with horizontal bands of Clipsham limestone, amid the courses of the darker local ironstone; a section of this masonry survives at the western end of the north wall, the rest having been refaced in a plainer manner.

As an aisled hall, it echoes the tradition of the

great timber-framed Saxon halls known now only by excavation; this tradition carried on well into the Norman period. Internally, the richly decorated stone arcades of the aisles are typical of the late twelfth century. The building is a fine example of the Transitional style, when the solidity of the Norman Romanesque developed into the more delicate Early English Gothic style.

The general style of the interior, the quality of the workmanship, the richness of the carvings and the capitals of the columns have been compared to the much grander work at Canterbury Cathedral. The work at Canterbury was begun in 1174 by one of the greatest masons of the era, William of Sens, and finished by William the Englishman after the first William was crippled after falling off the scaffolding in 1177. Perhaps Oakham had been built by

TOP: *The first walls beginning to appear in structures surrounding the Great Hall.*

ABOVE: *The exterior of the Great Hall, showing the length of our main trench traversing the external features.*

someone who had worked at Canterbury. An estimated date in the late eleventh century seems to be confirmed by the tree-ring dating of reused medieval timbers in the roof to the 1180s.

The original round-arch-headed entrance doorway was at the eastern end of the south wall, but was re-sited to a more central position in the nineteenth century, being swapped with a reset window. The paired windows in the aisle walls have pointed arched heads and colonettes with water-leaf capitals. This mixture of round and pointed arches is typical of the Transitional style.

The plan, like the architecture, was also transitional in another sense – a development from the separate hall and chamber block towards the composite hall with attached cross-wings and cross-passage at the 'low' end, away from the dais for the lord and his family at the 'high' end.

In this case, there is a proto-cross-passage from the original entrance, but rather than leading to an opposing door in the north wall, it seems to have ended in a stair against that wall instead. There is a setback for its landing in the masonry and round-headed doorways at both ground- and first-floor level in the gable wall.

Two other doorways, with pointed arches on the inside and round arches externally, are positioned centrally within the east gable and probably led to service rooms and perhaps a separate kitchen block beyond. There is a primary doorway at the northern end of the gable wall at the 'high' end, which presumably provided access into the lord's private accommodation. The hall would have been heated by an open hearth.

In a recent reassessment of the design of the Great Hall, Nick Hill suggested that it had primary tall timber-framed lean-to roofed sections attached to each gable, accounting for the rather poorer quality of the masonry of the gable

walls and distinct setbacks high up each wall, which could have taken the top plates of the suggested lean-to roofs. As the corners of the surviving building are neatly chamfered, and the plinths of the side walls return briefly on the gables, these extensions would have been slightly narrower.

The evidence of these additions makes sense of the doorways in the gable ends and suggests a fairly compact design. These timber-framed extensions appear to have been replaced later in the medieval period by masonry structures presumably performing the same roles – and removing virtually all archaeological traces of their predecessors. There was also a chapel close by, which had been rebuilt at least once, and was linked to the hall by a covered passage.

As well as being the communal heart of the castle's domestic accommodation, the Great Hall

ABOVE: *Despite the size of this trench, there were relatively few visible features. Note the presence of ranging rods to give a sense of scale in photographs.*

BELOW: *The exterior of the Great Hall, with windows in the early English Gothic capital style.*

would also have been the venue for hearing cases in the manorial courts. This role continued after the castle had become effectively redundant and slowly dismantled, and the hall became the main court for the manor and the diminutive county of Rutland. The fact that it was so well suited for such a purpose must have ensured this remarkable building's survival: it remained in use as a magistrates' court until 2001.

A key part of Nick's analysis was the fact that we should expect to find at the west end the living quarters of the lord – the lord's chamber, or, as it would be called later, the solar. Richard had identified a blocked doorway which would probably have provided access for the lord to get from the high table at the end of the hall to his personal rooms. This is the kind of building where we should expect to find some high-quality stonework and furnishings; once geophysics had been completed, this area would be the site of Trench 3.

Having completed an earthwork survey, Stewart had a good sense of where the main area of building might be. I asked him what he looked for having done his initial drawings (for a more detailed look at surveys, see the mini skills masterclass on page 108).

BELOW: *The geophysics survey laid over the plan of the Great Hall.*

HOW TO USE A TOPOGRAPHIC SURVEY

The various lumps and bumps distributed across the landscape are often strong indicators of past human activity. They can represent a variety of features, including ditches, moats, banks, mounds, roads, paths and ponds. These features are all divided into positive and negative types: positive being a build-up of archaeological material such as banks or middens; negative being those cut into the surrounding earth, such as channels cut by medieval traffic.

Most sites are a mixture of positive and negative types, which at first glance can often seem to lack form and pattern, particularly when they reflect a number of different phases of activity. Therefore, when archaeologists come across a promising site, great pains are taken to systematically measure, record and draw the various undulations. This type of work is known as a topographic survey, and by employing this technique it is almost always possible to make sense of these features and illustrate the relationship between both the features and the surrounding landscape. These accurate maps of the earthworks can be used to reconstruct plans of villages and field systems, and, perhaps most importantly, help archaeologists decide where to excavate for more information.

The first form of measured topographic survey was the Ordnance Survey (OS) maps, originally conducted for military purposes in the late eighteenth and early nineteenth centuries. These early maps were put to archaeological use by pioneer archaeologists such as General Pitt Rivers. By the early twentieth century, many of Britain's ancient monuments had been accurately mapped for the first time by

ABOVE: *Early maps and other documents from Oakham.*

archaeological surveyors such as O. G. S. Crawford.

During the creation of the Ordnance Survey maps, surveyors etched a series of benchmarks, consisting of a horizontal line with an arrow engraved underneath, across the country on buildings or other semi-permanent features. The height of each benchmark is calculated relative to the heights of others nearby in a nationwide network originating from a fundamental benchmark, which in turn is measured from the Ordnance Datum (usually mean sea level). The exact position and height of each benchmark can be found on the Ordnance Survey website.

Each surveyed site will have its own regular system of measurement and coordinates, known as a site grid. The corners of the site grid will be accurately positioned using the benchmark system. Developments in technology such as GPS systems and total stations (electronic instruments used to read slope distances) help archaeologists and surveyors to locate such information much more quickly, making the job less arduous than it once was. Within the site, measurements are taken from the corners of trenches, the positions of important finds or the elevations of earthworks. Each point should have a reading for east and north on a site grid with regular levelling measurement. These measurement points, which often number hundreds if not thousands, are used to build either a complete drawn plan of the site – an important and traditional model of presenting the data – or a digital map programmed with the site data.

Although the digitization of data has greatly helped archaeologists, when it comes to understanding and deciphering the landscape the old-fashioned method of notebook and pencil is hard to beat. The various features are drawn in three dimensions with the help of drawing conventions such as hachures, used to represent the direction of a slope and how steep it is. Hachures are strokes: the general rule is that steeper slopes are reflected by shorter, thicker and closer-together strokes; while gentler slopes are reflected with longer, thinner and further-apart strokes. This technique forms a type of shading and although they are non-numeric and so less useful to scientific surveys, hachures are extremely useful for communicating specific shapes of terrain. They are an extremely useful way of representing complex data for archaeologists trying to understand the complex relationships between the positive and negative features in the landscape.

LEFT: *Close-up of Stewart's notebook, showing how the lumps and bumps of the landscape are recorded by hand.*

On Day Two, with the trenches going well, Phil was beginning to find evidence of walls, but they went much deeper than we had thought.

WAS IT POSSIBLE that the structure that had been built at the east end was primarily of wood? John and Jimmy were still struggling to make sense of their radar plots. What was evident from the trenches was that a thick layer of clay was potentially obscuring the walls below – if there were any!

We had also begun to get pottery finds from the trenches. Jane Young, a local pottery expert, was on hand to accurately date the material. This greenware is the classic pottery from the medieval period and a common find on many sites from this time.

Accurate dating requires good local knowledge, however, and an expert can often tell us where the pottery came from.

The basic technique Stewart uses is to look for the earliest streets in the village, which can often be located by consulting early maps. The development of a market and the arrival of a Norman planned town with burgage plots creates distinct shapes in the village that can be seen either in the maps or from the air.

BELOW: *Phil and Tony discussing the contents of a trench at the edge of the site.*

LEFT: *Local pottery expert Jane Young working her way through the finds at Oakham.*

On Day Two Stewart was able to take advantage of the helicopter to look at the context of the Great Hall and the surrounding town. The areas outside the motte and bailey may well have had some kind of Saxon origin; there has always been a suspicion of a Saxon settlement in Cutts Court.

Finding Saxon artefacts has always been a tough task for archaeologists in general and *Time Team* in particular. Apart from burial sites, the building remains tend to be ephemeral, consisting of beam slots or brown stains next to slightly darker brown stains. Saxon pottery can be rather crumbly and has been unkindly referred to as looking rather like dog biscuits! For a more detailed look at Anglo-Saxon pottery, see Paul Blinkhorn's mini skills masterclass on page 78.

ABOVE: *Stewart and the helicopter team prepare for take-off.*

EARLY MEDIEVAL POTTERY

The breakdown of the Roman economy, with its networks for the large-scale distribution of goods by road and water, brought the end of mass-produced ceramics (fired in kilns) all over Britain. In most of the West Country, and in Wales and Scotland, the production of pottery ceased entirely, and for around 500 years (AD 450–AD 950) most people lived without pottery, using instead organic goods, mostly made of leather, wood, horn and bone.

In these areas of Britain, it was only in the late Saxon and Norman periods (between the tenth century and the twelfth) that people once again began to use pottery regularly in the home. At this stage, production was essentially a cottage industry, using local clays, and often made by rural potters working on the fringes of heathland or wasteland. Their pots were largely handmade, without using the wheel, and were fired in bonfires rather than kilns. Very little of this pottery was glazed, and most of it was completely undecorated. Nevertheless, it often shows a high degree of craft skill, sometimes with remarkably thin wares.

Due to differences in clays and firing techniques, these local coarse wares of the early medieval period vary greatly across the country. Some of the potteries of late-Saxon England must have been operating on a large scale, sending their wares 50 kilometres (30 miles) or more from their kilns. For example, evidence suggests that in the south-west of England one local coarse ware, made in the Blackdown Hills (known as Upper Greensand-derived ware) would have been exported to other areas of Devon. Similarly, in Bristol, which became a

ABOVE: *A late Anglo-Saxon lamp. The bowl would have been filled with oil, with a wick floating in the middle.*

major pottery manufacturing centre in the medieval period, potters were already exporting their wares to South Wales, Ireland and along the Bristol Channel.

The most ubiquitous forms of ceramics found on late-Saxon and Norman sites are cooking pots, with some bowls and pitchers. It has been suggested that the increase in these types of ceramics is linked to the rising popularity of boiled and stewed foods. Occasionally other more specialist items are also found, including storage jars, lamps, open bowls and spouted pitchers.

In these westerly parts of the country, it was

not until the late twelfth century that wheel-thrown wares came to prominence once more. At the same time as these handmade wares were being produced in most of Britain, potteries in northern France, the Low Countries and Germany were developing a more advanced technology of wheel-throwing and kiln-firing, sometimes using lead glazes, to produce attractive pottery. Unsurprisingly, continental pots of this kind were increasingly imported into Britain; in the south and west of England there was a marked increase in imports from France and particularly Normandy after the Norman Conquest, while pottery from the Rhineland found its way into East Anglia and London. Some of these vessels may be connected to the growth of the wine trade from the ninth to twelfth centuries.

By the late Norman period, fine glazed jugs from north-west France were proving to be very popular in the ports of southern Ireland and around the Irish Sea; they have been found in ports like Bristol and Dublin. These pots were beautifully glazed, had delicate decoration and used fine white or buff clays, which gave striking glazes. Unlike the handmade coarse wares being produced in Britain during the period, these French pots were being manufactured on wheels, making them finer than their British counterparts and thus more desirable.

See pages 118–19 for more examples of early medieval pottery.

John Allan

ABOVE: *An intact Norman gritty-ware cooking pot, thrown on a potter's wheel, with rouletted decoration.*

ABOVE: *Pottery and bone finds from Oakham. Note the obvious inclusions – probably pieces of small grit or shell in the pottery.*

Stewart's analysis of the town suggested that elements of its Saxon origin could still be seen:

There has been life and dwelling around the burh for at least 1,000 years. It is just fascinating the way life grows up around a stimulus. If you think of it like a single cell reproducing itself and continually growing until it becomes you or me, that's what the process reminds me of.

What we've learned is that as far back as AD 800 or 900 there was a royal Saxon burh here. It seemed to be quite prosperous even

then, as a Saxon queen called Aelfrith, who was the wife of Edgar, held Oakham around 964. A hoard of silver pennies – maybe as many as a thousand – from 980 were found in 1750, so someone clearly had a lot of wealth.

We think the hall would have been surrounded by farm animal barns like the one Tracey is working on, grain stores and storage. There would have been very little or nothing at all outside the surrounding defences. But the output from the hall would have attracted a market immediately outside the burh, and that would have continued to grow.

THE ARCHAEOLOGY OF A VILLAGE

All settlements go through a number of different phases of development. The best way to interpret these phases is by looking at the settlements from above, for example by using aerial photographs and historical maps. From above it is possible to view the different relationships between features such as roads, building plots or railway lines and establish which features may have developed earlier than others. A dramatic example of the way that features can be relatively dated by their relationship to one another is the course of the Roman road that runs past the ancient mound of Silbury Hill, near Avebury in Wiltshire. It was found that the road made a pronounced swerve around the base of the hill, demonstrating conclusively that the mound must have predated the construction of the road.

Although this Roman road is an obvious example, the same principle can be applied on a much smaller scale in order to establish the various relationships between features within a settlement. You will probably walk past many examples of later features respecting earlier ones every day in your local town or village. For example, when a street meets a town wall and changes direction, it is likely that the wall is either contemporary to or predates the street. By identifying interactions like these on a micro scale, archaeologists can create a list of each development within a village in chronological order.

Once the relative chronological order of the features within the settlement has been established, it is possible to group various developments into phases. This allows archaeologists to view the village on a macro scale by identifying the key developments that occurred within a particular time period. For example, locating all the alterations that reflect the development of narrow burgage plots will highlight the medieval phase of a settlement, whereas the concentration of plots towards the edge of a village during the 1870s could be attributed to the building of a railway station.

Settlements of different periods often share common features that help archaeologists to date them. A medieval market town, for example, will usually have a wider section of street where traders would have set up stalls to sell animals and often a prominent market hall. The core of a Saxon town is likely to be surrounded by a defensive enclosure or burgh, which will often survive in the pattern of the modern settlement. These key identifying elements often run along similar patterns. Learning to recognize these patterns – the residual parts – in contemporary landscapes is an important part of understanding the age of towns and villages and the way in which they have changed over time.

ABOVE: *Oakham village. The Great Hall is just beyond the church spire.*

On the final day we found more evidence of the lord's living quarters, including some fascinating bits of medieval roof tiles in the shape of a coxcomb.

SMALL PIECES OF Anglo-Saxon pottery continued to appear, and in the trenches we were able to date some of the walls to the period of Walkelin de Ferrers. I asked Cassie to summarize her thoughts about Trench 2, which had finally revealed a significant wall dating from the thirteenth or fourteenth century; see Cassie's view from the trenches on page 117.

Oakham had in many ways been a challenging dig, not helped by the difficulty of operating geophysics in poor soil conditions, but it had made us revisit some more traditional archaeological skills, which in its own way was fascinating. I asked Neil, as the chief archaeologist for this shoot, to summarize his thoughts:

Overall it was a puzzling, at times slightly frustrating dig. I was always hoping that the next trench would turn up clear traces of a building for which we could demonstrate a function and date. I don't think we should be disappointed by the results, though – we did plenty of good work which has characterized that high-quality archaeology still exists at Oakham, and if we had the time and money to open big areas we would doubtless reveal fascinating stories. I think this is just how medieval castle archaeology is.

Did I enjoy it? Absolutely – three days of pitting my wits against malfunctioning geophysics, tricky archaeology, plus trying to keep Phil sweet, were great fun. Many archaeologists would have loved to have been in my shoes, so I was lucky to be there. Oh, and the pub just outside the gate was really nice – I enjoyed having a few pints with Phil and John and catching up on the gossip.

RIGHT: *Chief archaeologist Neil and the rest of the team take a well-earned break.*

CASSIE

When we arrived at Trench 2, it was fairly obvious that we were digging a substantial earthwork! Stewart's survey had located what looked like three sides of a building. As we watched Ian taking off a thin layer of turf, we could begin to see rubble underneath, which looked hopeful. Not nice squared-off stones like the building behind us, but often a building can be demolished or robbed out and we only get the foundation level. After two to three hours of clearing and digging, we had what looked like a rather jumbly pile of yellow stones. Was it just a garden feature put up in the post-medieval period?

As we took off more of the topsoil, we began to find the odd piece of pottery that looked like thirteenth- or fourteenth-century greenware, which was encouraging. But as usual, this wasn't from the wall itself but the soil around it. These finds were all carefully put in the finds trays, to be collected by Wessex Archaeology after being identified by the pottery expert.

As we excavated further down the wall, we were looking for evidence of the construction cut that was dug to create a base for the foundation. A critical part of dating these features is to look for dating material in this area and within the stones that make up the wall itself. While digging we had to keep a careful eye out for any of the small pieces of pottery. Tracey, who was supervising the trench, was keen to get to these lower levels, but she was perplexed by what appeared to be a layer of clay packed around the wall.

By Day Two we had a number of pieces of thirteenth- or fourteenth-century pottery, and intriguingly some small sherds of late Anglo-Saxon wares were appearing although in the general subsoil. To distinguish between the pottery that is residual – that would have been in and around the soil that the building was placed in – and the material associated with the building is a critical part of the excavator's skills.

By the end of Day Three, Tracey was fairly certain that we had a building contemporary with the Norman hall, but its purpose remained enigmatic. At least the dating gave us a sense of satisfaction. Also we were able to show Stewart what was under the earthwork that he had drawn two days earlier!

One of the key pottery finds: a medieval pot base from Cassie's trench.

EARLY MEDIEVAL POTTERY: 1066–13TH CENTURY
Some typical examples and how to identify them*

1. Blackdown Hills cooking pot (Upper Greensand-derived ware)

Among the most common finds on late-Saxon and Norman archaeological sites in south-west England are fragments of handmade unglazed pottery. The most common vessels were cooking pots, although other forms have also been found, including lamps, storage jars and lids. The pots pictured here are thought to have been made around the edges of the Blackdown Hills, at the border between Devon and Somerset. Studies of the pots' fabrics have shown that the coarse filler used to temper the clay contains minerals such as flint, limestone and quartz, with some pieces of fossilized shell – a link to the parts of the region where fossils derived from Cretaceous rocks are found. This fabric type was used as early as AD 950 and continued to be used until the early fourteenth century.

2. Glazed tripod pitcher

This glazed tripod pitcher was also made in the potteries of the Blackdown Hills. The pitcher was found on an excavation in Bartholomew Street in Exeter and has been dated to AD 1150–AD 1200. Jugs were comparatively rare until the late twelfth century; their introduction may have been due to new ways of presenting drink at table, or changes in dietary habits or methods of storing drink. This vessel was handmade and acquired the name 'tripod pitcher' due to the addition of three short and stubby feet to the base of the pot. The pitcher would have been used for carrying and storing liquids; evidence from a variety of sources including the Luttrell Psalter suggests that people may have carried this type of container over one shoulder.

3. Imported glazed ware – western French jug

This imported jug is of French origin and has been dated to the end of the twelfth century. Its precise provenance remains unknown, but similar jugs have been found in excavations in Orléans, so the source may be somewhere in the Loire Valley. The jug was clearly thrown with great skill and made with very fine white clay. Its body is scored with triangular shallow grooves, over which a mottled green lead glaze has been laid. Its brilliant colour was achieved by mixing small amounts of copper (probably in the form of bronze dust) into the glaze. The jug is the only complete example of its sort ever found in England, although sherds of others have been discovered during excavations in Dublin and Southampton.

4. Wheel-thrown Normandy gritty ware cooking pot

In the ports of southern England, another commonly imported ceramic was Normandy gritty ware. Pots such as these were wheel-thrown, rather than handmade, and generally had pale, buff-coloured bodies, often sooted over time by use. These types of pots were characterized by their shape, including an upright collared rim, as well as their distinctive quartz inclusions. Archaeologists believe they originated from the region around Rouen in northern France, the Norman heartland. Unlike most English coarse-ware cooking vessels, these pots were wheel-thrown, and they sometimes display simple decoration such as rouletting – a pattern impressed into the pot's surface with a roller.

This particular selection of examples is typical of western Britain.

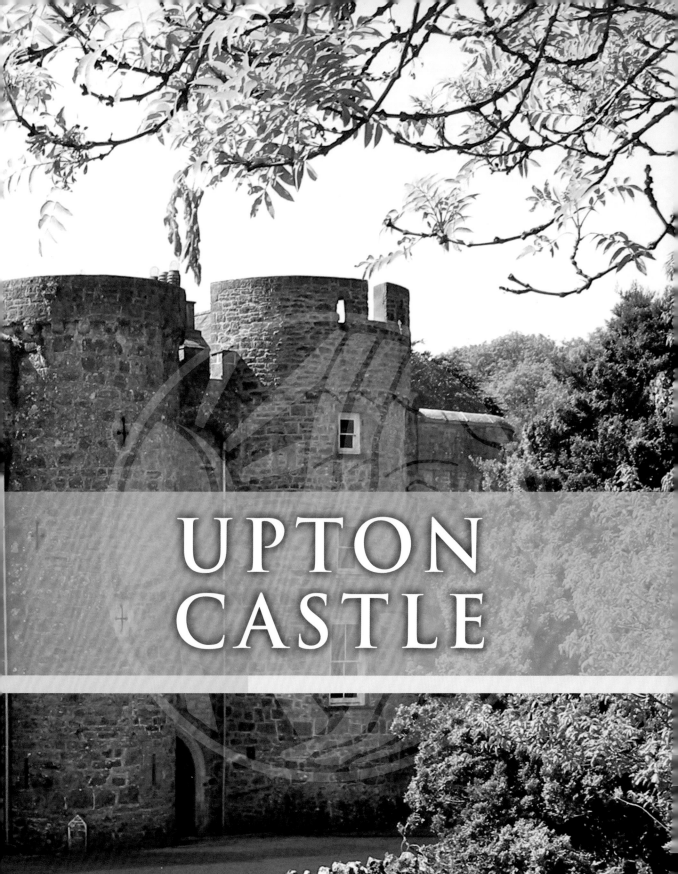

UPTON
CASTLE

Upton Castle in Pembrokeshire is believed to date back to Anglo-Norman times, from around the thirteenth century.

THE TOWERS, ARROW slots and vaulted ceilings all point to Norman origins, but later changes had made it harder to recognize which elements were original and which were later embellishments.

Prue and Steve Barlow had fallen in love with Upton and bought it as their home in 1997. They wanted us to confirm which were the genuine key medieval features, and also to date and establish the origins of the beautiful chapel adjacent to the castle, which appeared to be on a slightly different alignment.

The project design defined the key archaeological goals. Upton is Grade II listed and the gardens around the castle are of historic importance. We liaised carefully with the CADW inspectors and the inspector for historic parks in order to clarify the areas we could access and those areas that we would need to protect.

Research aim 1: What are the character, extent and function of surviving archaeological remains comprising the thirteenth-century castle thought to have been built by Sir William Malefant?

RIGHT: *The grand entrance to Upton Castle. Above the door can be seen the two chain holes for the drawbridge, and other features which may or may not be original.*

OPPOSITE PAGE: *Looking down into the back courtyard with the team in action. This area had been considerably disturbed and built up, which made it difficult for us to find features.*

TONY'S PIECE TO CAMERA

" Castles in Wales: they're symbols of warlords, princes, sieges and bloody battles … But this week we're at a castle that's right off the beaten track, known to be a real mystery. Welcome to Upton Castle in Wales, where even the current residents are in the dark about its history.

We've got a free rein to dig this place, and it's a tall order. We need to find out who built it, when they built it, and why.

This could be one of the biggest challenges we have ever had. But one thing we can be sure of is that something over 700 years old will have a fascinating story behind it. "

Research aim 2: What are the character, extent and function of surviving archaeological remains comprising pre-Anglo-Norman settlement at the site?

Research aim 3: What are the character, extent and function of the apparently 'ruined building' within the grounds of Upton Castle: are they contemporary with the main castle build?

On Day One the main targets were to see if we could find a moat on the front drive that would support the idea that the drawbridge features were real. Phil would be starting work in the cloister area at the back of the castle. From the plans, it appeared that the castle should have had a range of buildings closing off a cloister area. One disadvantage from the start was that the geophysics seemed to be having difficulty seeing beneath the tarmac on the drive.

With the diggers trying to make sense of the initial trenches, it gave us a chance to look into the historic background with

HOW TO EXCAVATE A SITE

On most excavations, the basic principle is that each new soil layer is completely removed before proceeding onto the next. This kind of 'layer-cake' technique is called the stratigraphic (or context) system of excavation. Although not all digs adopt this process, it is the most common system followed by archaeologists.

Slowly stripping away each layer of soil takes a great deal of patience and care. The goal is not to dig as deeply or as quickly as possible, but rather to fully understand the sequence of the activities that have taken place at the site. A context, also known as a feature or stratigraphic unit, is a distinct archaeological entity, such as a rubbish pit, a post hole, a depositional layer or a ditch. A site will generally contain many successive layers of material that have built up over hundreds or even thousands of years as a result of human activity. Archaeological evidence is frequently left behind by those who lived on the site, trapped in the different layers of soil. Therefore, when excavating, it is vitally important to keep all of the soil from each of these layers separate, in order to reconstruct exactly what has happened on the site in the correct order.

It is crucial to understand that while excavation is a process of retrieving and understanding the hidden archaeology, it is also a process of destruction. Once a site is excavated, it can never be restored and so is gone forever. The site then only exists in the field notes, recording forms, photographs,

ABOVE: *Phil carefully excavating a site. Note the range of tools and the grid on the right used to help record a feature.*

drawings, reports and publications. Therefore, as soon as you begin an excavation, it is your responsibility to ensure that everything is conducted to the highest possible standards, preferably by involving a professional archaeologist. It is always better to dig a smaller test pit that is well excavated, accurately recorded and fully published than to undertake a large, poorly managed and unpublished excavation.

Using a hand trowel

Archaeologists use a whole range of tools during their work, but one of the most important is the trusty hand trowel. Trowels are used both to define the outline of a deposit and to expose or remove it. Both the texture and consistency of the soil affects the type of trowelling technique. If the deposit is sandy or loose, then it is best to scrape the soil away with the edge of the trowel. However, if the soil is hard and compacted, the only option may be to carefully break it up with the point of the trowel. Never use the trowel to randomly hack away at the soil. Sometimes a site will contain lots of large, fragile artefacts, such as shell. In these cases, it is better to remove the deposit in chunks, rather than risk breaking artefacts with the trowel.

When scraping, always use the long flat edge of the trowel and pull it towards you, so that the excavated material doesn't get pushed back onto the newly exposed surface. This scraping technique is often used to clear up and tidy the base of each soil layer before a photograph is taken. In order to trowel efficiently, your weight needs to be over the trowel, so it is better not to sit down while you dig. Always keep a dustpan and bucket handy so that you can keep removing the excavated soil from the trench.

When an intricate, delicate or fragile find is uncovered, archaeologists use small brushes to clean off the soil. Small brushes and excavation tools, such as a dental pick or lollipop stick, are useful for cleaning out small cavities. A lot of evidence for past human activity will be incredibly subtle, such as stains in the soil, which may indicate the use of charcoal fire, or decomposed timber posts. This information could be easily missed if care is not taken during the excavation process. If a discolouration in the soil or another unusual feature is uncovered, best practice is to carefully clean back the area using a light scraping technique or a brush. Never keep trowelling, as you run the risk of damaging the feature. Working slowly and carefully is the key, as even small changes in the physical characteristics of the soil could be of great importance.

ABOVE: *Phil using a brush to excavate pottery on an Iron Age site.*

Suzannah Lipscomb, who had been searching through the historical documents. One of the earliest Norman owners may have been a family called the Malefants (or Malenfants), and from the start hanging onto their castle had been a challenge for them. Access to the south of

ABOVE: *A small filled-in window in the chapel, perhaps indicating an earlier date.*

Pembrokeshire had been relatively easy at the start of the Norman invasion, particularly given the proximity to the Bristol Channel, but the local Welsh lords were well organized and belligerent.

A programme of castle building was begun to create a chain of defensive sites that would also impose Norman control over the area. These structures were some of the most advanced military architecture seen in Britain up to that day; castles like Pembroke and Carew were massive and impregnable. Upton was on a smaller and less ambitious scale, but it played its part in creating a fortified ring around the south coast of Wales. Suzannah was able to find a reference to Upton, or Openton as it was then called, paying rents to its neighbouring castles in 1362.

In 1406 Upton played a role in the battle against Owain Glyndŵr, who was fighting for Welsh independence. Along with a number of other castles, it had paid into a fund to bribe

ABOVE: *The top floor of the ruined section is misleading. The pointed window is Victorian and there were two upper halls: the present floor is inserted and the ladder on the left is supported on the corbels of the original top floor.*

Glyndŵr not to attack Pembrokeshire.

Back in the trenches, Phil and Raksha had begun to see the base of what might be an early doorway, while Cassie was turning up seventeenth-century pottery – tin-glazed earthenware. The doorway had a rebate on the inner face. In Trench 3 at the potential moat site, the hard surfaces below the drive tarmac looked to have little signs of a steep-sided ditch that might hint at a moat, so a decision was made to extend the trench. The lack of a moat led the team to take a more critical view of features like the chain holes above the entrance. In the incident room Emma was able to show us the results of her LiDAR survey, and this with the trees stripped away showed more clearly how the castle was sited on a valley, with access to the river and the sea beyond at Milford Haven. The valley in medieval times would have provided a good source of power for mills, which could 'if time permitted' be another good target for us to pursue.

A selection of pottery finds from the courtyard area.

HIGH MEDIEVAL POTTERY

During the thirteenth and fourteenth centuries (an era sometimes referred to as the 'late' or 'high' medieval period), there was a major decline in the production of pottery cooking pots, no doubt reflecting the rising use of metal vessels in cooking. A shift occurred in wealthier households of the period, especially those in towns: where once stews would have been cooked in ceramic vessels upon a fire, the majority of cooking now occurred in metal cauldrons suspended from the chimneypiece. On the other hand, there was a growing demand for colourful earthen tableware, especially jugs, and in some areas other types of vessel such as bowls came into widespread use. The more unusual vessels produced during this period

include lamps, small dishes, dripping pans and fire covers. This was a time when decoration became more prevalent, with multi-coloured effects and applied decoration.

Kilns were brought into general use for producing jugs and other tablewares throughout Britain during the thirteenth and fourteenth centuries. This development meant that higher firing temperatures and greater control could be achieved; this was especially important for the production of glazed wares.

The import trade in ceramics from the Continent grew significantly during this period. Jugs in particular were being imported, of varying shapes and with a range of differing decorations to satisfy the changes in fashion. Particularly striking is the trade in imported pottery from the

ABOVE: *A medieval cooking pot recovered from an isolated farmstead in Dartmouth, Devon.*

Saintonge, an area just north of Bordeaux, which developed during the mid-thirteenth century. This can probably be linked to the rising wine trade from Gascony. These jugs would not have carried the wine, which came in barrels, but they would have been used to serve it at table. With their dazzling colours these vessels must have been very striking features of prosperous medieval homes.

The lack of small individual metal or glass mugs dating from this era suggests that these jugs would have been used for communal drinking. This is in sharp contrast to the later Tudor period, when a large number of drinking mugs were imported from the Low Countries and France. This shift is a reflection of the change in custom from communal drinking from large jugs to individuals being served drink in separate mugs.

By the end of the middle ages, new types of pottery were emerging, some of them connected to the rising demand for cups for individual drinking – for example Midlands

ABOVE: *A green-glazed medieval jug, made in Saintonge, France, but recovered by archaeologists in Exeter.*

purple ware, a near-stoneware ceramic with purple fabric, which usually has a pimply texture and a dark, sparse glaze. These products were made in multi-flue kilns, allowing for better control of the temperature within the kiln. This removed the need for sand and grit inclusions, which were previously used to prevent cracking during firing, meaning that potters were able to produce fabrics from finer clay.

See pages 140–1 for more examples of high medieval pottery.

John Allan

Day Two began with a geophysics survey of the land around the chapel. Neil took the decision to accept that no sign of the moat could be found.

THERE WERE TWO good targets in the chapel area, where we could see a blocked doorway and a point that would tell us more about the extension to the chapel. It was possible that the chapel predated the castle, so anything that Phil could discover could be crucial.

Cassie and Rob were persisting with their courtyard trench, but it looked as though much of the original structure had been either dug away or covered with layers of late infill.

Suzannah had been able to identify one of the effigies in the chapel as being that of a Malefant, possibly Sir James, who had died in 1362. From other information she was able to suggest that the castle could have been occupied by Malefants in the late fourteenth century, but there was a suggestion of an earlier connection, possibly the De La Roche family, who in 1200 had married into the Malefant line.

Critical to our understanding of the castle was the work of Richard K. Morris, our buildings expert, who had been working his way around the house from Day One. Richard's hard work in hunting through the existing building for traces of its earlier past had paid off handsomely. He was able to confirm that inside the large two-storey,

ABOVE: *Jimmy out with the radar, still looking for signs of the non-existent moat.*

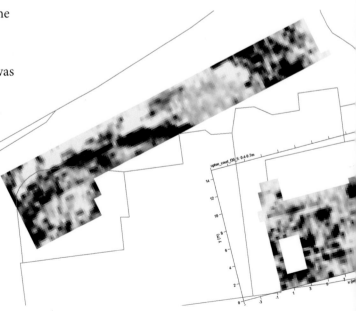

RIGHT: *Geophysics results from around Upton Castle.*

BELOW: *Victor's reconstruction of a solar in a medieval hall, complete with fireplace, from an earlier Time Team programme.*

barn-like room behind one of the towers were traces of medieval fabric, including a fireplace in what may have been a solar, or the lord's main chamber, and large stone supports for the crossbeams of a medieval floor. He also felt more certain about the original drawbridge architecture once he had seen the tracery around the holes used to take the drawbridge ropes or chains.

Despite the lack of a moat, it was possible that a drawbridge had once covered a deep pit, preventing easy access to the main entrance. Richard summarizes his work at Upton in the mini skills masterclass on page 132.

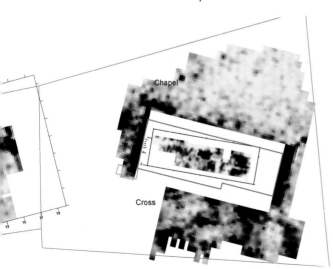

Chapel

Cross

ABOVE: *Computer-generated reconstruction of the winding gear for lifting the portcullis or drawbridge.*

HOW TO ANALYSE BUILDINGS

The most important thing in archaeology is to not have any preconceptions about the site. This logic still applies even when the archaeology is above ground, for example a standing building. So when we come to excavate a site, we will often ignore what the project brief says and instead focus on understanding the building and its surroundings. At the Upton site, initially we began by trying to figure out how much of the building had been altered. This work became more and more critical after the various archaeological trenches around the castle revealed little about the castle's development.

The first step was to have a good look inside the building. Various parts of the building were closely examined, such as the joist pockets in the walls, the levels of floors, the fireplaces and the spiral staircases. This then gave us a good idea of what we were looking at: a three-storey lodging with towers and spiral staircases – a building of a very high status. After establishing this, we were able to knock some of the preconceptions about the site on the head. For example, previously it had been suggested that there was originally a doorway at first-floor level, in the front of the castle. This didn't make any sense in the context of the building being a castle. We found that, in fact, there were two doorways to the back of the castle, which made the evidence from Trench 3 much clearer. This is one example of how we began to unpick the various mysteries surrounding the castle.

We also had a look around some of the domestic parts of the castle that are still in use. Here we found traces of a much larger structure, as well as bits and bobs of medieval fabric. This showed that the castle was originally a very large complex, possibly with a central courtyard. Unfortunately, the archaeological investigations could not locate the other parts of the courtyard walls. This was possibly because the area in which we were digging had been heavily terraced, probably during the Victorian period, which had wiped out most of the medieval elements.

Another interesting aspect was the possible drawbridge at the front of the castle. There were two clear holes in the wall above the entrance. It seemed likely that these holes would have been built in order to accommodate drawbridge chains.

LEFT: *The top of the well-crafted spiral stair in the central tower, linking the upper floors with the battlements.*

ABOVE: *Each of the upper halls was heated. This is one of the original fireplaces, with the blocked reveal of a window opening to the left.*

The holes had rather neat quatrefoil outlines, which appeared to be genuine rather than faked. In addition, upstairs above the entrance there was a chamber that could have been the winding chamber for the drawbridge. Unfortunately, it had been partly rebuilt, and so it was impossible to see the internal view of the drawbridge holes. The evidence appeared to show that there had once been a drawbridge. However, when a trench was put in beside the entrance, there was no evidence of a moat. Rather than a moat, it seems likely that there would have been a drawbridge pit.

In some respects, the chapel was even more interesting than the castle; it became the key to understanding the site. From the start, I was fairly convinced that the chapel was much older than the castle. The chapel's proportions and the opposing doorways towards the west end of the nave suggested that it may have once been a little Norman chapel that had later been altered and extended. If so, this meant that there was possibly a settlement on the site predating the castle. The critical clue to proving this theory was locating the apse. If the chapel had been built before the castle, during the Norman period, we would expect it to have had a semicircular apse at its eastern end. In order to investigate this further, we looked at a sketch plan of graves within the church. There was a clear lack of graves inside the church in the area where the apse might have been – and then geophysics seemed to find a solid baulk of semicircular masonry in exactly the right place. Unfortunately, we were unable to dig it up, as this discovery was made at around 4 o'clock on Day Three! However, the evidence seemed to point towards the conclusion that the small chapel would have been the oldest building on the site.

Richard K. Morris

As Cassie and Rob worked on in their trench on Day Two, it turned out to be a rather nice example of, as Cassie put it, 'upside-down stratigraphy'. The top layers had thrown up pottery from around the sixteenth or seventeenth century, and beneath these a range of nineteenth-century building rubble had turned up, including house bricks! This illustrated the importance of archaeologists clearly being able to define the stratigraphical layers, preferably down to the natural or bedrock. How is it possible to be sure you are not dealing with this kind of 'false' stratigraphy? We explain more about this process in the mini skills masterclass on page 136.

Someone in the eighteenth or nineteenth century had brought in a load of topsoil from elsewhere on the site and used it to level up the cloister garden. An excavation or test pit in the top 70 centimetres (28 in) or so would have led to the erroneous conclusion that this area was *circa* sixteenth century. The early drawings of the castle showed that the grounds had been radically remodelled and this introduced material from elsewhere. One clue to this was the nature of the top deposits, which were less stratified and more mixed and disturbed, a possible clue to the redeposited nature of the material.

Neil Holbrook clearly found Upton a frustrating site; by the end of Day Two the goals of finding the moat and the cloister had receded into the Welsh rain. However, Phil had been able to figure out the relationship between the chapel and its extension, showing in section that the smaller building foundations 'rode up' over the earlier building's structure.

The main archaeological focus was now the chapel and its burial ground. Could this at least give us some clue to the site's origins? By this point, we had put in more than ten trenches, including one in the walled vegetable garden, to see if a circular earthwork might be the early boundary of the church. Phil, who had moved onto a trench in the central burial area, had found some stained glass, which might hint at the way the chapel was decorated in medieval times.

The rather battered effigy in the chapel may well date to a period earlier than that of the Malefants. The style of the armour and the crossed limbs, indicating a knight who went on

LEFT: *Finds liaison officer Danni Wootton examining a cannon ball found in the grounds.*

ABOVE: *Showing Prue and Steve the radar results from the chapel.*

the Crusades, may date back to the twelfth century.

Our conclusions about Upton as presented in the final film left me feeling a little uncomfortable. We had concentrated on the chapel on the final day and made considerable progress in dating the site, the burials and showing that the nave was a later addition. Quite how this related to the castle is a moot point. The chapel could represent an early Christian site, or a structure related to a much earlier settlement than the castle. The origins of the castle may relate to a desire to utilize an already occupied site, so knowing the dates of early burials in the churchyard doesn't necessarily help us to determine when the castle was built.

USING STRATIGRAPHY

The sites archaeologists excavate may have been produced over a long or short period of time. Occasionally, sites can be the remains of a single event, such as a mound of rubbish left behind after a lavish feast. The process of archaeological excavation assumes that the order in which the site has been laid down will reflect the sequence of events that occurred at the site over history. The deeper you dig, the older the archaeology. This is known as the principle of superposition, which is the fundamental basis for stratification. Stratification is the process of sedimentary layering and its observed result, while stratigraphy is the archaeologist's interpretation of the stratified layers in words or drawings.

Unfortunately, on most archaeological sites, it is rarely that straightforward. A huge variety of complicated factors interfere with stratification. These can include natural processes, such as wind, floods and rodents' burrows, which can deposit or remove material. Later human activity, such as digging ditches, can alter or remove evidence of past events.

The principle of association assumes that items found together within the same deposit are essentially of the same age. However, this must always be applied with caution. Some items remain with a family for many years, such as an heirloom passed down from generation to generation before being thrown away; such items may be much older than the other materials within a layer. The principle of reversal applies when deposits have been removed and redeposited on the same site but in a different order. Material is rarely dug out and placed on the same site, rather than being moved elsewhere; but this can occur after major construction work. The principle of intrusion states that an intrusion will be more recent than the deposit through which it cuts. Underground ovens, rubbish pits, foundations for walls and ditches are all intrusions into the older deposits around them.

All excavation is based around these three principles. Through extremely careful removal of each layer and detailed attention paid to its colour, texture and contents, an archaeologist can successfully reconstruct and understand the past sequence of events at the site, both natural and human. However, not all sites are stratified; some may have no visible stratification. The site may have been created by a single event, such as rubbish being dumped. In these cases, excavating using stratigraphy would be useless.

ABOVE: *A neatly marked-out trench: each layer is given a specific figure which will be referred to in the report.*

Day Three saw Tracey in Trench 6, working her way down in the pouring rain. The large natural boulders at the surface eventually revealed a grave cut, and in Phil's latest trench – number 8 – we would find further grave cuts.

ABOVE: *The first trace of bones in the chapel area.*

THE CONTEXT FOR Tracey's burial, which appeared to have been cut down to the bedrock and to contain relatively little later material, suggested an early date; these bones were sent off for radiocarbon dating, the results of which gave us a date of around 1250. Tracey's trench was probably one of the most important on this dig. For Tracey's thoughts on the excavation at Upton, see her view from the trenches on page 139.

On this final day, John and Jimmy began to scan the chapel floor with radar to see if any features were hidden underneath. The chapel contained some fine medieval features, including the effigy of William Malefant (who died in 1362) and a font. Was it possible that there were more features to be found? Towards the end of the day, they were able to show that there could well be other burials hidden beneath the chancel and, more importantly, that the chapel may originally have had an apse. The results appeared to show a curving semicircle adjoining the point where the chancel and nave met. It seemed possible that an apse had been removed at the time when the extension was added.

Prue and Steve were clearly delighted by this latest development, and Richard's identification of the key medieval features would, we hoped, inspire them to carry out more renovation work and perhaps research to find out the identity of the mysterious burial under the chapel floor.

LEFT: *Summarizing our finds at the back of the castle.*

USING RADIOCARBON DATING

Radiocarbon dating is also known as carbon-14 dating (C-14), after the carbon isotope upon which this dating method relies. Three principal carbon isotopes occur naturally: C-12, C-13 (both of which are stable) and C-14 (mildly radioactive or unstable). All organic matter contains a tiny amount of C-14, acquired during growth. As C-14 is radioactive, it decays (changes into another element) in a consistent and measurable way. When organic matter dies, tissue no longer obtains any fresh carbon, including C-14, so the presence of the element begins to decline. Measuring how much the C-14 fraction has declined is how scientists are able to determine the age of organic matter.

A group of scientists led by the late Professor Willard F. Libby were the first to develop radiocarbon dating techniques at the University of Chicago in 1949; Libby was later awarded the Nobel Prize in Chemistry for his work. From its early development, radiocarbon dating has evolved into an essential technique within the field of archaeology. Any material composed of carbon can theoretically be dated, from charcoal, bone, wood and seeds to wall paintings, textiles, hair and pottery. Another huge advantage of the radiocarbon method is that it can be uniformly applied throughout the world. The method can measure, within a reasonable degree of accuracy, dates up to 10,000 years ago, and can also provide useful dating information for up to 40,000 years ago. However, it does entail fairly wide margins of error – between 50 and 100 years.

Properly calibrating radiocarbon dates is essential. The levels of carbon-14 have varied in

ABOVE: *Tony showing the bone that would be sent for radiocarbon dating, eventually dated to around 1250.*

the atmosphere throughout time. For example, levels of carbon-14 within the atmosphere have been elevated since the detonation of atomic bombs in 1945. Radiocarbon dates therefore need to be calibrated with other dating techniques in order to ensure accuracy. Dendrochronology (dating using tree rings) is commonly used to calibrate radiocarbon dates. At the Upton site, a radiocarbon sample was taken from the burial in Trench 6. The dates were calibrated and showed the person died around cal AD 1010–1160 – the 'cal' prefix indicates that the dates are the result of radiocarbon calibration using tree-ring data.

Radiocarbon dating cannot be carried out on site. Samples of organic matter to be radiocarbon dated should immediately be placed in a plastic finds bag and kept away from contamination, such as human skin or cigarette ash, which could significantly affect the result. An apparatus known as an accelerator is used to extract the carbon in a laboratory. The procedure is very expensive, and samples can take several weeks to process.

VIEW FROM THE TRENCHES

TRACEY

One of the first things that became apparent at Upton Castle was the level of landscaping that had taken place there, largely during the Victorian period. This is fairly commonplace, so it wasn't a surprise, but it boded ill for any possible surviving archaeology. Indeed, the first trench I was involved in proved to be empty, with no sign of the possible moat the experts had hoped might have existed. But my second trench was placed near to the wall of the chapel in an area of lawn, and this proved far more interesting. The chapel itself was a lovely small private chapel, with later additions to its Norman core. We thought it likely that there would be evidence of burials, but nothing remained (such as headstones) to suggest their locations, so three trenches were placed to investigate both the construction of the chapel and whether any burials survived outside the building.

To begin with, the nature of the geology on the site confused matters, as the fracturing of the bedrock looked surprisingly like manmade walls. However, one of the local archaeologists recognized this as being a natural formation for that area; this was a good example of the value of using local knowledge on *Time Team* sites.

It was only after further exploratory excavation within the trenches that we uncovered the first of a small number of skeletons, one of which I worked on. Even when you expect to find skeletons on a site, I still find it fascinating to uncover the previous inhabitants of a site. There is always something quite moving about excavating human remains: it is, after

all, the most direct link you can have to the previous occupants of a site. I removed a small fragment of bone for dating from the skeleton. Once this was recorded, we recovered the remains and restored the ground above them to the peacefulness of the grassy lawn, the quiet of the chapel and the company of the resident cat, who had kept a watchful eye over our three days of digging.

LEFT: *Tracey examining a small find.*

HIGH MEDIEVAL POTTERY: 13TH CENTURY–15TH CENTURY

Some typical examples and how to identify them

1. Exeter striped jug

During the latter part of the thirteenth century, good-quality wheel-thrown glazed ceramics were being made over most of the British Isles. These would have been the classic tableware of the late medieval period. These attractive striped jugs are a common find at Exeter. Archaeologists believe the vessels shown above were made in the immediate area around Exeter, although the exact location of the kilns has not been determined. Some of the Exeter striped jugs have vertical striped decoration; on others the stripes are horizontal or curved. In order to achieve this look iron filings were rubbed into the clay, making black stripes that contrast very nicely with the orangey-red colour of the glaze. This glaze was created by oxidization during the firing of the pots, creating the orangey-pink colour.

2. Saintonge jug – green glazed

Around the mid-thirteenth century, a new pottery tradition was established in the Saintonge, the area around Saintes in south-west France. In contrast to the common red ware and earthenware of England, this tradition used very fine white clays, which were thrown on the wheel. They were so delicate that many of the pots must have smashed during the journey to England. The majority of the output consisted of fine jugs, with a glaze of brilliant green; this colour was achieved using powdered copper. It is believed these jugs were used for serving wine at the table; people probably drank communally from them. Later, in the Tudor period, it became more common for people to eat and drink from individual plates and glasses.

3. Fourteenth-century floor tile

Floor tiles were sometimes made in separate kilns, or sometimes fired alongside the pots. At first, floor tiles were found only in sacred buildings or very wealthy households. For example, in 1300 only the king and some churches and monasteries would have been able to afford tiled flooring. As time passed, floor tiles filtered down the social spectrum, and by 1500 townsmen and possibly a few others would have been able to afford to have them in their homes.

4. London ware jug with sgraffito decoration

In the mid-twelfth century a new pottery industry developed in the London area, supplying well-made and brightly glazed wheel-thrown jugs to the capital. At that time most other parts of England were still using handmade pottery, so this new tableware proved popular and it was widely distributed by coastal trade; examples have been found all along the south coast of England as far as Cornwall, and along the east coast up to Scotland. Some vessels, such as this one from Exeter, were made in the North French style – that is, they copy the shape of pottery from Normandy, with a tall ribbed neck, rod handle and bright decoration, achieved here by using a white clay slip and combing down to the body – an example of the sgraffito (scratched) technique.

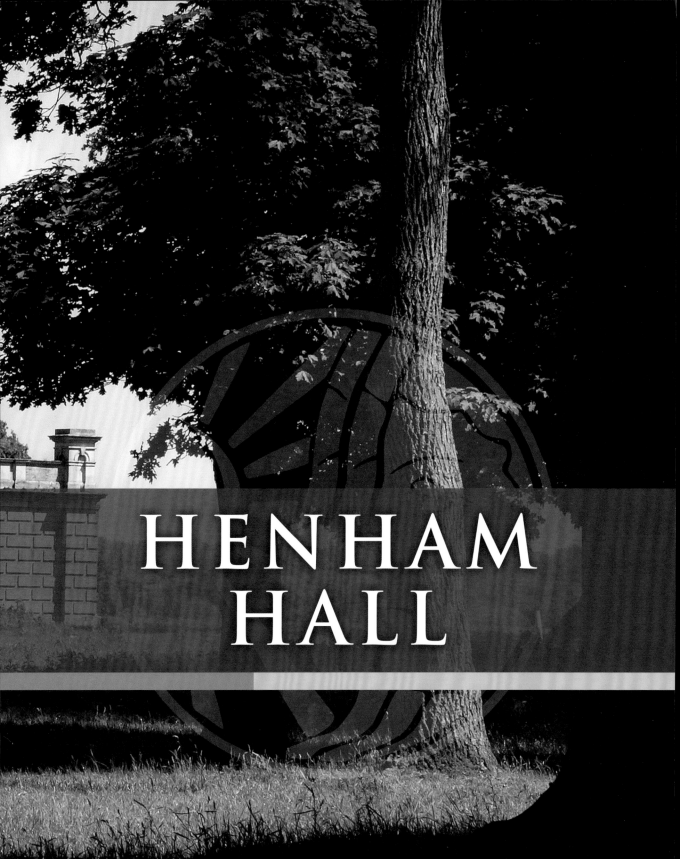

HENHAM HALL

Henham Park in Suffolk is a 330-hectare estate containing the remains of a number of historically important grand houses, including a Tudor hall built in the early sixteenth century by Charles Brandon, Duke of Suffolk.

The Duke of Suffolk and Mary Tudor.

THE DUKE WAS a close friend of Henry VIII and went on to marry the king's sister Mary Tudor in 1515. At eighteen, Mary had been married to the fifty-five-year-old Louis XII, and through this first marriage she became queen of France. Her second marriage to Charles Brandon (his third) was possibly more of a love match. The couple married secretly in France, at great risk: technically it was treason to marry a royal princess without getting the king's assent.

Despite this Charles continued to be a favourite of the king, and this led to him being granted the dukedom and vast lands and buildings in Suffolk. He moved into Henham in around 1524 and from that period on began modernizing and expanding the house and gardens.

In 1538 he was relieved of his property by the king, following pressure from Thomas Cromwell and others. At this time, Henham was described as having a new gatehouse with four turrets and two good parks. The Rous family acquired the estate in 1545. The first of the line, Sir Anthony Rous, was an important member of court and the keeper of the royal Jewel House.

ABOVE: *Remnant of the Georgian mansion at Henham, pulled down in 1953.*

Henham Hall was destroyed by fire in 1773 and a new house was subsequently erected: a Georgian mansion built to designs by James Wyatt around 1790, which was pulled down in 1953. The later building has never been excavated. A remnant of it, a brick loggia originally attached to the new hall, can still be seen in the parkland.

Due to the historical importance of the whole site, Jim Mower had spent some time discussing the strategy and project design with English Heritage inspector John Ette, the team leader for the East of England, who has worked on a number of projects with *Time Team*. John's advice and cooperation have proved invaluable on many occasions.

The Henham estate is now run by Hektor Rous, who had invited *Time Team* to uncover

LEFT *Henham Park from the air. The main area of our work was to the left of the walled garden.*

TONY'S PIECE TO CAMERA

❝ Rumour has it that on the night of the eighth of May 1773, a butler crept into his master's wine cellar while he was abroad, to steal his finest claret. Worse for wear from drink, he was accused of dropping his candle and setting not only the cellar ablaze but also burning down the entire house, which had stood since Tudor times.

Welcome to the magnificent Henham Park in Suffolk: beautiful parkland, mature trees, red deer – but no trace of a Tudor mansion.

Fleeing the scene, the butler was never heard of again, but the house that he supposedly burnt down is under here. Does it rival the finest Tudor house in England? That's for us to find out. ❞

more evidence about its lost buildings. Hektor was working as a banker in Australia when he inherited the management of the estate, after his grandfather died and his father passed it on for him to run. Hektor has a real passion for the Tudor period; the magnificent Tudor mansion that dominated the estate in the sixteenth century would be a key target for him. The original mansion had been destroyed under mysterious circumstances. Tony focused on this in his opening piece to camera.

The project design we prepared in advance set out the research aims for our work, which were as follows:

Research aim 1: How has Henham Park changed in layout and appearance over time?

Research aim 2: Is the 'linear pond' close to the dairy farm buildings the remnant of a

moat surrounding the Tudor house, or evidence of an earlier medieval house on the site built by the de la Pole family?

Research aim 3: What is the character of subsurface archaeological remains comprising the Tudor-period Henham Hall?

Research aim 4: What is the character of subsurface archaeological remains comprising the Georgian-period Henham Hall?

A side product of destruction by fire for archaeologists is that burning can increase the magnetic responses in the walls of the building. When objects are burnt, the original magnetic signature is removed and then reacquired in a way that makes the signal more coherent and stronger, and therefore more easily detected by

LEFT: *The roof of the Land Rover is a popular location for our cameramen.*

the geophysics. To improve our chances of getting a clearer plan of the buildings, John had brought along state-of-the-art MALÅ ground-penetrating radar (GPR) equipment, which over the course of this year's series had really proved its worth. With seven sensors and eight antennae, the radar was capable of producing high-resolution images. It would give Jimmy another chance to charge up and down in his favourite JCB utility vehicle, adapted to pull the radar and to serve as a base for the GPS system.

With Francis Pryor in charge of the archaeology, we wasted no time in setting John, Jimmy and the team to work. The critical goal was to try to locate the dimensions of the structure on the ground, which would enable us to target those features most diagnostic of a Tudor building. We have worked on a number of Tudor sites before, and the key features tend to be the central gateway and the corner towers. These often require substantial foundations and therefore could be the easiest to date and to locate in the ground.

DIGGING AND MANAGING A SMALL TRENCH

Positioning your trench is very important. You will need to check the area for signs of underground services, such as drains and cables, and make sure to avoid them. Pre-excavation work (see the mini skills masterclass on page 176) will help evaluate the best position for a trench.

Access and spoil

Making sure you have good access around your trench is essential so that work can be carried out safely. Spoil heaps can soon grow much larger than you would expect, so always allow for expansion. Position spoil at least 1 metre (3 ft) from the trench edge for safety, but not too far away, as you'll have to backfill the pit eventually.

Starting to dig

Once you've decided where to dig, you need the correct tools: a measuring tape, string, nails, a spade, a trowel, a shovel and a bucket. The first step is to mark out your trench using string and nails. Dig up to the string and not beyond it. Try to get the spade under the turf so that there is an even thickness of soil left under the grass. This will make it easier to re-turf once you've backfilled the pit. Stack the turf at a sensible distance from the edge of the pit, grass to grass and dirt to dirt, making sure not to cover the turf with spoil.

Digging a trench is a three-dimensional activity, so don't just concentrate on the bottom of the trench: make sure you keep the sides of

RIGHT: *An example of a small trench at Oakham.*

the trench clean and vertical and keep an eye out for different archaeological layers. Your trench should always be the same size at both the surface layer and the bottom layer. As Phil Harding says, 'good diggers are clean diggers', so keep your trench tidy and clean up your loose dirt as you go. That way you are more likely to be able to spot finds and identify new archaeological layers – the 'stratigraphy' or chronological sequence of deposits.

Always remove the soil slowly and carefully, keeping an eye out for separate layers within the soil. You may notice a new layer because it's a different colour, is harder or softer, contains more stones or is different in some other way. It may cover only part of the trench, in which case it might be a feature like a pit or post hole. Don't go

Finds

In any trench you are likely to encounter a variety of finds, including pottery, coins, worked flint and other datable pieces, but also look out for bones and shells, which can help in understanding dietary activity in the past. All finds should be put in bags marked with the site code, trench number and layer. It's always worth keeping anything you're not sure about; items can always be discarded later once they have been looked at by a specialist.

Recording

Recording the trench is one of the most important aspects of the archaeological process. If you are not prepared to do the recording, you might as well not dig the trench in the first place. The trench must be photographed, the section drawn, and context numbers assigned to each layer and annotated on the drawing. Finally you need to describe the layers within your trench, answering questions like: is it sticky or dry? What colour is it? Does it contain lots of sand or clay? Are there stones? How many? What size? What are they made of? It is also worth continually trying to interpret the trench throughout the digging process. For example, how did the soil for each layer get there: was it through natural or manmade processes? How did a find reach this point: was it deliberately buried or accidently discarded? Interpretation is a skill that archaeologists learn through experience.

Finally, your trench must always be located on the main site plan, showing its position relative to fixed points such as the corner of a house. This is an incredibly important part of the process, allowing finds to be accurately plotted on a map and recording the exact location of your trench for future researchers.

Steve Thompson, Wessex Archaeology

ABOVE: *A typical selection of finds from the trenches at Brancaster.*

down any further, but clean the bottom of the trench and call for an archaeologist; they will need to see the hole looking nice and tidy before they can tell you what to do next. It is vitally important to keep finds from different layers in separate bags; if you encounter a feature, any related finds should be kept separately too.

We decided to use the initial geophysics results to position two trenches as soon as possible: the first trench to be opened by Phil, in the area we hoped would reveal the gatehouse, and another one to be dug by Raksha on the corner tower. By the end of Day One, Phil was not convinced that he had located the gatehouse. The structure didn't seem to be substantial enough, and it became clear that we needed to revisit some of the later results that the geophysics team were processing. Raksha's trench seemed to be showing an equally uncertain set of evidence and was looking more like a ditch. However, she and Matt were finding substantial chunks of decorative Tudor brickwork, including fragments of a beautiful Tudor rose surrounded by the sun's rays. These kinds of Tudor mansions were built to display the owner's wealth and power and also presented an opportunity to illustrate one's loyalty and love for the crown, so lavish decorations like this were popular.

The Duke of Suffolk was one of the most important people in Tudor England and would have been aware of the symbolism of the Tudor rose. He was a hunting companion of the king. The duke would eventually leave Henham, but in his time the house must have been the setting for entertaining members of the court, including the

ABOVE: *Some of the Tudor brickwork remains were very close to the surface.*

LEFT: *One of our best finds: a fragment of the decorative brickwork showing the Tudor rose, which would have graced the exterior of the mansion.*

Hektor Rous, Henham's owner, and Suzannah Lipscomb talking history with Tony.

king himself, mounted in the greatest opulence and style that Tudor England could provide.

We had invited Suzannah Lipscomb, *Time Team*'s historian and an expert on Tudor England, to provide the background history to this fascinating site. Among the many ancient documents that made reference to Henham she was able to find lists of the contents of the mansion in 1602: a probate inventory included musical instruments, velvet-covered furniture, grand tapestries and displays of hunting equipment (including perches for hawks). It was fascinating that on the first day the archaeology revealed just a hint of the decorative splendour suggested by the terracotta Tudor rose.

At the start of Day Two, it became clear that we had positioned the initial trenches to the west of the key targets, and we would need to work further to the east.

AS OFTEN HAPPENS on archaeological sites, we had managed to put a massive spoil heap right over the location of our next trench. Once this was moved out of the way, Tracey could begin targeting the area where we now believed the gatehouse to be.

Both Phil's and Raksha's trenches were continuing to produce finds, including pottery that Paul Blinkhorn, our pottery expert, identified as late Essex redwall from around the fifteenth or sixteenth century.

Stewart Ainsworth now began a survey of the wider environment of the mansion. With Hektor on board, Stewart undertook a tour of the site and was able to locate a potential driveway, which would have originally been one of the main entrances to the mansion. The wide hollow way he found had possibly been created in medieval times, but then adapted in the Tudor period to create a tree-lined entrance to the site.

Tracey's new trench soon began to reveal structures that related to the gatehouse. The most significant evidence was a rubble-filled roadway that passed between two brick-built structures. This gave us the width of the entrance of the mansion.

Back in Hektor's current house, we were able to take a look at a remarkable scroll, which showed his family tree and the key members of

ABOVE: *Francis Pryor and Phil discussing strategy at the end of Day One.*

ABOVE: *Cassie cleaning up the surface of one of our early trenches. It's possible that this brickwork had been reused.*

BOTTOM RIGHT: *Included in the small finds was this Tudor hammered coin.*

his family associated with the buildings we were hoping to excavate.

By the afternoon of Day Two, we had begun to locate the Georgian mansion. Matt put in a trench to find its exact position on the ground. The geophysics results and the photographs and other material identifying this property would mean that relatively little work would need to be done; but, as on all scheduled sites, useful information about the condition of the architectural remains is important. This was particularly the case given Hektor's plans to

develop a new hotel somewhere in the vicinity.

Rob Hedge had also started working on an area of exposed brickwork, potentially part of a garden feature. The parks and gardens at Henham are a very important aspect of the archaeology, and any new information we could add would be valuable.

Towards the end of the day, our small finds expert Danni Wootton was able to identify a silver hammered coin from Rob's trench as being from the Elizabethan period, dating from 1575.

When Henham's Tudor mansion burnt down, one of the few objects to be saved was a wassail bowl, used to toast the assembled Tudor lords. We had decided to recreate one of these, with Matt trying his hand at using a pole lathe.

Suzannah's hunt through the documents had produced a really useful ground plan of the mansion. We also had a document from 1538 that included a description of '*a faier newe howse well buylded with tymber and fayer lyghtys and at the cumming in to the Court a faier yate howe of breake newly buylded with iiii turrettes*'. In addition, it seemed that by the end of Day Two we had managed to establish the exact width of the original house. This came as something of a surprise, because from the drawings, illustrations

TUDOR POTTERY

By the Tudor period (1485–1603), ceramic cooking pots had almost entirely vanished and serving jugs also became rather less common, to be replaced by metal counterparts. Instead, one of the most common ceramic finds from Tudor sites is a large open bowl. These bowls normally had a prominent lip, so it has been assumed that they were used to hold some kind of liquid, but archaeologists are unsure as to the exact purpose of these vessels. Many have been found where dairies were located, suggesting that they may have been used for activities such as clotting cream.

During the early sixteenth century, all sorts of new shapes of pot began to come into fashion. These tended to reflect the way in which the households of the early Tudor period operated. Increased trade led to a more European-style of eating and drinking within Tudor England. This foreign taste resulted in the introduction of a variety of new ceramic vessels, such as chafing dishes: these were the sixteenth-century equivalent of hostess trolleys and could be used for slow cooking or for warming water in which to wash one's hands.

Kiln technology was becoming more advanced during the Tudor period. In Germany and the Low Countries potters were now able to make stoneware, and this proved very popular throughout England. Earthenware is actually very porous; modern flowerpots are made from this type of fabric, as it allows moisture to drip out from the soil. However, for the purpose of transporting something like wine, or serving drinks at table, this quality is very inconvenient.

During the very late medieval period, some German and Low Countries potters found that a higher firing temperature created smaller gaps

ABOVE: *A Tudor drinking jug, complete with metal lid. The jug is made from Siegburg stoneware.*

between the inclusions in the clay: basically the clay particles were being melted more closely together. Using a variety of techniques the firing temperature was gradually pushed up over the decades. By the early fourteenth century, potters were achieving temperatures of around 1,150 degrees Centigrade, and by the fifteenth century around 1,250 degrees Centigrade. At this temperature, pottery is much less porous – a fabric type that became known as stoneware. Only certain clays were resilient enough to endure such high temperatures.

This development altered the industry in the Rhineland, as not all places were able to produce stoneware locally, so areas with this facility became massive production centres, producing pots on an industrial scale. The traditional lead glazes also could not endure these higher temperatures and instead everything turned black, creating a very unsatisfactory product. Instead, it was discovered that salt could provide an effective glaze finish. Salt glaze was also easy to make: all that was needed was a shovel full of salt, introduced to the kiln when it is at its hottest. The salt then evaporates and covers every surface it is exposed to. This creates the characteristic greyish-brown colours of glazed stoneware. Around the end of the sixteenth century, it was discovered that cobalt could also withstand the high temperatures. The use of cobalt provided the classic blue colour that became very popular towards the end of the Tudor period.

The introduction of stoneware cups neatly illustrates the shift during the Tudor period towards individual place settings at table. Instead of there being a large vessel from which everyone would drink communally, the wine would now be poured into smaller individual cups. Many famous paintings depict this transition, showing the fifteenth-century family sitting down to eat a meal using individual knives, forks and cups. By the fifteenth century, this change appears to have occurred across the whole of Britain, apart from in the West Country and Wales.

See pages 164–5 for more examples of Tudor pottery.

John Allan

ABOVE: *A Tudor bowl excavated from a kiln site in Exeter. The bowl is similar to pottery finds from the Low Countries dating to this period.*

BELOW: *Victor's reconstruction of a celebration at Henham Hall.*

and description we had imagined something much bigger.

This was an interesting example of how the archaeology in the ground can deliver accurate dimensions in a way that other evidence cannot. What had also begun to appear in the trenches was material suggesting an earlier building on the site that may have been incorporated into the Tudor mansion. Paul was able to identify Thetford ware from the thirteenth century: the amount of these finds, along with other documentary evidence, suggested the existence of a substantial

OPPOSITE PAGE: *Turning the celebration cup at Henham: our woodwork expert Stuart King showing Matt how it's done.*

RIGHT: *The top of a small bell found by Tracey in her trench.*

medieval hall here in the thirteenth century.

Day Two ended with a rethink of our strategy by Francis. We decided to see if we could find evidence of the earlier structure. Some nice small finds were starting to appear from the trenches, including a book clasp in Raksha's trench and the top half of a small bell, possibly from a horse harness. We are often asked about the care and treatment of finds and where they end up after a *Time Team* shoot. Wessex Archaeology explain what happens to the finds in the Appendix on page 216.

ABOVE: *Henham gave rise to some complicated trenches, all of which had to be recorded for the final Wessex report.*

WORKING WITH A COMMERCIAL CONTRACTOR

Wessex Archaeology, one of the largest commercial archaeological practices in the UK, has been involved with *Time Team* since the beginning, through the secondment of Phil Harding. In 2003 our involvement deepened when we were asked to provide a full back-up service for the team, making sure that sites were recorded to the proper standard, that finds were recovered and treated correctly, and that the results were made available in a report for each site. This was a very important step, indicating that *Time Team* were learning from the archaeological profession that the recording and dissemination of their results were just as important as actually digging them. It's a fact that is central to archaeology in general: if you dig but don't make records or tell anyone what

you find, then you might as well not dig in the first place. Archaeology is destructive, so you can never go back to a site as it was.

So for the last twenty years we have been supplying two people to attend each *Time Team* dig: one to record the trenches (you can read Steve Thompson's account of how this is done on page 148); and another to make sure that all finds are collected and labelled correctly, and to supervise any volunteers who might come along to wash the finds.

Then the real work begins. This is the part that the viewing public don't generally see, although there may be short clips of various specialists working behind the scenes. In contrast to the very pressured three days spent filming the site, this process can take anything up to a year or more to complete. We have to coordinate a number of different pieces of work, from the initial period of sorting out the site records and making sure they are complete, through the process of gathering various specialist reports (finds, geophysical survey and so on), to the final drafting of the report and illustrations. The report is a technical document which includes descriptions of the archaeological deposits encountered, and their interpretation, the finds, and the contents of the sieved soil samples. It is submitted not only to *Time Team* and the landowners, but also to the archaeological department of the local planning authority, and sometimes to English Heritage too. Most of our completed reports are also available via the Wessex Archaeology website (www. wessexarch.co.uk), and this has proved to be one of the most frequently viewed parts of the site. The key here is accessibility: although our reports are technical documents, they should be available not just to the profession, but to the general public too.

We run our *Time Team* sites just like any other project, with budgets, timescales and 'deliverables' stated in advance; however, as we work mainly within the commercial sector, there are certain differences in approach which we've had to be aware of and work around. From the beginning, our aim has been to do the best we can by the archaeology, within the given constraints. This is the same on any commercial archaeology site, and it is a fact that the pressure we face on some of those projects (housing schemes, road schemes and so on), in terms of time and resources, is similar to what we've faced while working with *Time Team*. I'm happy to say that I think we've managed to maintain our high standards of recording and reporting throughout.

Primarily, of course, we've had to adapt what we do to fit in with filming. Recording has to be fitted in so that it doesn't interfere with pieces to camera – if our recorder is working in a trench

while filming is taking place, then for the sake of continuity they may have to stay there until filming finishes, however long that might be! Our finds staff have to keep track of finds in their often complicated journey from initial discovery through various episodes of filming and specialist examination on site.

Overall, our many years of working with *Time Team* have been extremely happy ones, and I think both sides have benefited from the experience. We have helped to give the programme archaeological credibility, and this has helped enormously in negotiations for access to certain sites. In return, *Time Team* has provided our staff with opportunities to work on sites of a widely diverse nature – including a Second World War site from German-occupied Jersey, an early post-medieval metalworking site in an inaccessible part of the Lake District, a Napoleonic prisoner-of-war camp in Cambridgeshire – many of which they would rarely have had the chance to visit in the course of normal commercial archaeological work. We are proud to have been involved and hope that we've helped to make a difference.

Lorraine Mepham, Wessex Archaeology

ABOVE: *A small collection of finds. Note the careful numbering, which means they can be matched up with specific trenches for the report.*

ABOVE: *Raksha's trench, showing the deep ditch that Stewart identified as a potential moat.*

Fortunately we were able to get Richard K. Morris, *Time Team*'s buildings expert, to look at the plans of the medieval hall.

RICHARD WAS ABLE to suggest that at the rear of the Tudor mansion there may well have been the remnants of an earlier structure. This theory, combined with the geophysics scans, gave us a target for what would be the final trench. The aim would be to locate the back range and any other information about the Tudor period kitchen that was believed to be in this area.

In Raksha's trench it became clear that she was dealing with a huge ditch, and after discussions with Stewart it seemed possible that this was a moat that had once surrounded the medieval building. Stewart began to survey both the depth of Raksha's trench and the depth of other features

on the site, including a large narrow lake behind Hektor's current house. His conclusion was that all these features seemed to be approximately the same depth and probably represented the remnants of a huge medieval moat.

Phil was able to proceed quickly with the trench on the back range. By lunchtime on Day Three, he was able to show Tony a number of finds that related not to the medieval period but to the Tudor kitchen. It became clear that the depth of material represented evidence of a huge cellar. Among the finds were molten lead, window glass buckled by the heat and twisted fragments of pewter.

These items clearly appealed to Tony as potential evidence for the disastrous fire. Fragments of Italian marble and other architectural remains showed the high status of the interior of the Tudor Henham Hall. On the final day it appeared we had found evidence of the three major mansions on the site. We had been able to give Hektor an idea of the grand style in which his Tudor ancestors had lived.

The Henham programme was rich in historical documents, maps and illustrations, but what was particularly interesting for us was how the critical pieces of evidence were provided by the fragments of pottery, particularly Paul's identification of the medieval Thetford ware, and finds from the trenches that revealed the exact dimensions of the Tudor buildings at Henham. These structures were perhaps not quite as grand as Hampton Court, but Henham was certainly a place fit for a visit from the king and the home of a duke, husband to Mary Tudor, a former queen of France. The terracotta Tudor rose surrounded by symbolic rays of the sun perfectly encapsulated the richness of Henham's story. It was one of the iconic finds of the dig and will doubtless find a place in *Time Team*'s list of greatest-ever finds.

ABOVE: *Richard K. Morris showing Tony the potential location of the medieval building.*

LEFT: *The team enjoying a beer on the final day at Henham.*

VIEW FROM THE TRENCHES

ROB

I must admit that I approached this site with a certain amount of trepidation. Could we really shed new light on the story of the site? The destruction of large buildings tends to create a lot of debris, which can hamper the efforts of the geophysics team – in geophysical terms, a surviving wall and a patch of rubble can look very similar! Demolition debris also takes a lot of time to shift.

My fears were unfounded: Jimmy's new toy produced the goods, plenty of elbow grease put paid to the rubble, and it was one of those happy instances where lumps and bumps, documentary evidence and holes in the ground all came together to enhance our understanding of a site.

Once geophysics had completed their initial sweeps on Day One, we set about investigating a curious line of brickwork that protruded just above the turf to the south-east of the walled garden. We removed the turf by hand and then set about exposing the structure. It became increasingly clear that it was a curving wall, beginning at a solid square brick pillar at the western end of the trench. The wall was constructed from a single skin of bricks laid end to end. The curvature and slender brickwork, combined with the presence of a wavy line on a plan of the Georgian house, enabled us to identify it as a 'crinkle-crankle' wall, characteristic of the Suffolk area. The wiggly outline gives the structure stability, doing away with the need for buttresses. As well as looking striking, these walls were economical – the strength imparted by the shape allowed them to be just one brick in width. Even taking into account the extra length due to the curves, this represented a considerable saving in the numbers of bricks required!

As we exposed the lower levels of the wall, another intriguing quirk became apparent. Although the wall itself appeared to be eighteenth century, the platform upon

ABOVE: *Rob and Danni Wootton discuss the small finds from Henham.*

which the wall sat was constructed from unmistakably Tudor bricks. Some of the demolition material from the ruins of the burnt Tudor house had been reused in the Georgian structure, though the salvaged bricks would have been hidden below ground, out of sight. More rubble removal followed, and just as we were starting to think we'd never get below the demolition debris, we hit sand, cut by the unmistakable outline of a backfilled 'robber trench' – bang on the projected line of the wall of the Tudor house!

ABOVE: *Rob in action backfilling a trench.*

Moving on to Phil's trench after Day Two, I cleared yet more rubble from the interior of the backfilled cellar. The ubiquitous jumble of broken bricks was broken up by some lovely finds among the debris, including fire-buckled and twisted window glass and lead, a German jetton, or gambling token, and a coin fashioned into a love token by careful bending into an S-shape. Finds like the love token really appeal to archaeologists as a rare glimpse into the personal, emotional dimension of the past.

With time running out on Day Three, I helped Matt to expose remains of the Georgian house just a couple of inches below the turf. As the rain came down after lunch, I began to record the walls and surfaces we'd uncovered. Each trench is meticulously recorded and hand-drawn, and where there are complicated structural remains the drawing can be very labour-intensive. Some archaeologists heartily dislike recording, but I love it! The process forces us to be systematic about our conclusions.

As exciting medieval discoveries were being made elsewhere, I was left with my drawing board and a trench full of walls. I was able to consider the meaning of what we'd uncovered. A drain had been crudely cut through the impeccable Georgian brickwork. A close inspection of the mortar and pipe suggested the work had been done, badly, in the early twentieth century. Was this an indication of ad hoc repairs as the price of maintaining the building spiralled? Or the work of an unscrupulous tradesman, unaware that his shoddy workmanship would be exposed a century later? We can't be sure; but that tiny footnote to the history of Henham Park is one that no documentary source is likely to record, and that, in a nutshell, is the beauty of archaeology.

TUDOR POTTERY: 1485–1603
Some typical examples and how to identify them

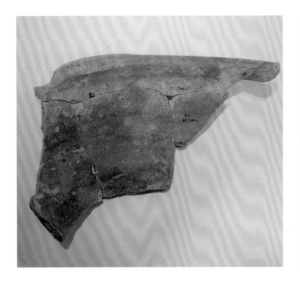

1. Big open bowl – pancheon

These big open bowls are one of the most
common ceramic finds on a rural Tudor site. The
vessels were very large, some as wide as 25
centimetres (10 in) across, with sloping sides and
a flat base. It appears the pots were prone to
cracking during the firing process, so the potters
created heavy rolled rims around the edge to
strengthen the pot. The pots were glazed on the
inside – a typically post-medieval characteristic.
The prominent lip and internal glaze suggests the
pots may have been used to hold some kind of
liquid. Many examples have been found within or
near dairy farms, suggesting they may have been
used for clotting cream. Another possibility is
they were being used to cook, as some finds have
shown traces of soot from a fire.

2. Bellarmine jug

Bellarmine jugs are also sometimes known as
Bartmann jugs, a decorated type of stoneware
manufactured throughout the sixteenth and
seventeenth centuries in western Germany. The
jugs are characterized by their unique decoration:
a bearded face applied to the neck of the vessel.
Additional adornments included floral and
oak-leaf decorations or coats of arms. The jugs
were produced in a variety of sizes and for a
multitude of uses, including transportation,
storage and the decanting of wine.

3. Stoneware cup – Raeren vessel

This stoneware cup is dated to c.1480–1550 and is believed to have originated from the potting town of Raeren in eastern Belgium. These vessels are characterized by their light-grey or bronze-brown surfaces, achieved by using a salt glaze. The cups were fired to a much higher temperature than their earlier counterparts. This created a fabric known as stoneware, which was much less porous than the earlier earthenware. This find from Exeter reflects a change in the manner in which food and drink were served at the table in Tudor England, as individual drinking cups were adopted to replace the medieval practice of communal drinking.

4. Maiolica from northern Italy

Tin-glazed ware also became popular during the Tudor period. The production of pottery using this technique originated in the Islamic world, across in the Middle East, and spread to Spain and Italy. The addition of tin to the lead glaze created a brilliant white opaque surface, excellent for painting on. The pots were often painted with bright colours; the early designs tended to be geometric or with motifs of flowers, leaves, tendrils or fruit. Perhaps the most beautiful exotic pottery on the market in the Tudor period was Italian maiolica. During the fifteenth century these items were very rare, becoming more popular in the early sixteenth century.

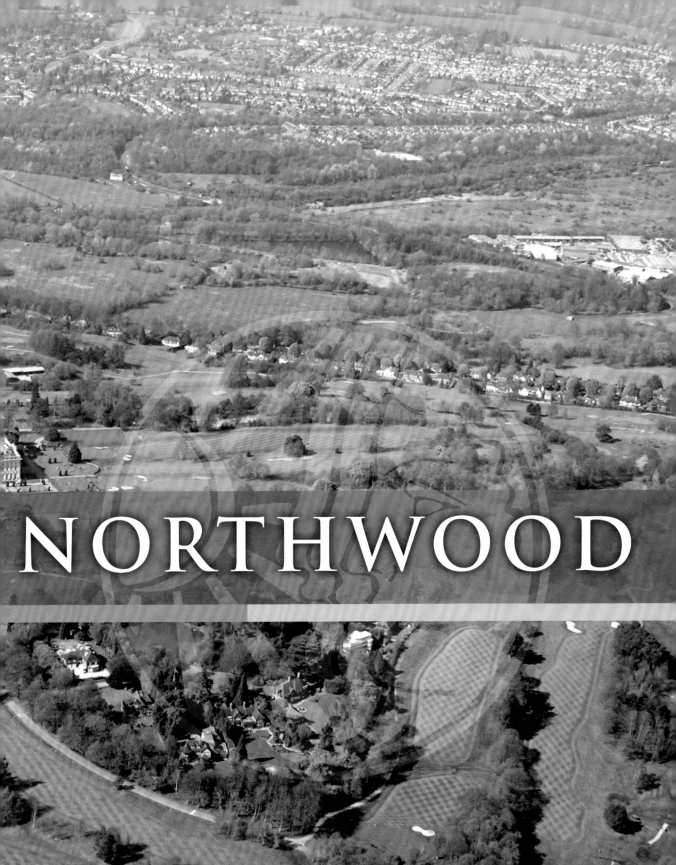

NORTHWOOD

Before we'd even arrived in Northwood, I felt that we were heading to a site where a really fascinating moment of history had taken place.

NOT ONLY WAS this the home of Cardinal Wolsey, chief advisor to Henry VIII, but it had also played a defining role in the life of Henry's first wife, Catherine of Aragon. For two years she lived here, still queen of England, but suffering the pain of Henry's displeasure as he sought to remove her in favour of Anne Boleyn.

Catherine's failure to produce the required male heir (the unfortunate woman had numerous miscarriages) and the king's infatuation with Anne Boleyn saw her gradually moved aside. The none-too-subtle method Henry employed was to gradually move her away from the mainstream of court life, sending her to locations further and further away from London. In addition, her personal court of attendants was progressively diminished. For a queen of England this must have been intolerable; however, when she arrived at Northwood early in the sixteenth century, she managed to preserve her status. Northwood was a palace near Rickmansworth and came to be known as the Manor of the Moor.

When Catherine entered through the grand gatehouse she was accompanied by over 200 courtiers. This was the scene that I would be asking Victor to recreate on the final day of the

RIGHT: *Pupils at Northwood Prep get an introduction to archaeology at one of our trenches. Steve Thompson from Wessex is concentrating on recording the trench.*

RIGHT: *Lead archaeologist Jackie McKinley is joined by John and Phil as they discuss the location of trenches with Professor Martin Biddle on Day One.*

shoot. The question was: how much of the palace still remained, and how much could we find to help inform the background to Victor's picture?

Northwood is now a rather grand preparatory school, and we wanted to involve the school and staff as much as possible. After all, it would be their playing fields we would be digging up! The headmaster, Dr Trevor Lee, was keen to find out about Northwood's illustrious past. Over the three days we would be managing the shoot around the school grounds, so the enthusiastic cooperation of the staff would be invaluable.

Northwood is also a scheduled ancient monument, so from the start we had close contacts with Deborah Priddy the local English Heritage inspector. We had worked with Debbie before and had established a good working relationship with her. Northwood is a very high-profile site for English Heritage because of its historic importance.

A key member of the team would be Professor Martin Biddle, one of the 'great and good' of English archaeology. Martin had dug on this site as a fifteen-year-old boy: he had gathered together a group of friends and persuaded the owners to let him carry out some small-scale excavations on key areas. This gave us a flying start. It's fair to say that Martin has had an almost obsessive interest in Northwood, so his work on documents, drawings and other information concerning the site would be invaluable.

With Martin and Debbie's help, Jim had drawn up the project design, which highlighted the key questions.

Research aim 1: What are the surviving extent and layout of the building complex and landscape features within the scheduled area in relation to the episodes of infill and demolition in the past?

Research aim 2: What are the location, extent and survival of the Outer Court (Base Court) and any associated buildings?

Research aim 3: What are the location, extent and nature of survival of the Long Gallery?

Research aim 4: From where did the More Portal elements originate?

As usual, Tony's opening piece to camera provided us with a simplified description of what we hoped to do in our allotted three days.

Before we got started, we had a chance to look at two rather beautifully carved columns that the gardener at Northwood had found buried in the undergrowth. Later, Kent Rawlinson, our architectural expert and the historic buildings curator for Historic Royal Palaces, would give us a detailed analysis of these features, but even at this early stage we could see the quality of the carving. The columns offered a tantalizing glimpse of just how grand Northwood must have been. The surface of each column was covered with palms and leaves surrounded by acanthus leaves, a pattern that represented the height of

ABOVE: *Within a fairly short space of time the school's playing field had been transformed into a series of trenches.*

TONY'S PIECE TO CAMERA

> **"** We're in search of a lost Tudor palace that was rumoured to be more splendid than Hampton Court – that's a huge claim. It once belonged to Cardinal Wolsey, King Henry VIII's chief advisor, and it lies here somewhere beneath the playing field.
>
> But the reason the school are going to let us dig up their best-laid turf is not just to find Wolsey's lost palace, but to see if the rumours are true. Was this really grander than Hampton Court? **"**

Renaissance style at the time.

From our research we knew that there had been an earlier palace built in the reign of Henry VII, and Wolsey had embellished this and added some grand design ideas of his own, including a Long Gallery 100 metres in length, which it was claimed could even be used for archery practice on wet days! When we later worked out the extent of the boundaries, it became clear that the estate stretched to over 600 acres of land, which in Henry's time would have contained deer for the king's sport.

In 2011 the school had commissioned John's company to do an initial survey and it was interesting to see the magnetometry or 'mag' results (see mini skills masterclass on page 173) and also to have John's interpretation. This is the kind of document that we often don't have time

to look at on *Time Team*. Using his experience, John interprets the geophysics scans, suggesting which elements might be walls, ditches or other features, and his contribution is always helpful.

We began by 'geophysing' the playing-fields area. Our hope was that the initial mag results covering the area outside the 2011 survey would lay out the main locations. We needed to establish the courtyard with its formal entrance and the Outer or Base Court. We already knew that Wolsey had both a Great Hall and a chapel.

The problem with many Tudor sites is that the stone is often robbed from the buildings. The fancy stonework of the palace was a great attraction to locals and there was a good chance

ABOVE: *Jackie checking the geophysics results.*

USING MAGNETOMETRY

Magnetometry (often abbreviated to 'mag') provides an image of subsurface features for archaeologists to interpret. Various ancient activities, such as burning, leave behind a magnetic trace, which can be detected using an instrument known as a magnetometer.

Burning, be it deliberate or accidental, permanently changes the magnetic properties of the surrounding soil by altering the magnetism of tiny iron particles. The soil around features will give either higher or lower readings: deposits containing little burnt material, such as stone walls, will normally be lower; while features with higher amounts of burnt material, such as ditch fills and pits, are usually magnetically higher. Kilns and metal-working areas result in very strong and characteristic anomalies. Occasionally, bacterial action can alter the magnetic properties of the soil, although this normally occurs in wet soil conditions and can therefore be a useful technique for locating old rivers and lakes.

The magnetometers used during geophysical surveys will often have two (or more) sensors to measure the gradient of the magnetic field (essentially the difference between the two sensors). Known as fluxgate gradiometers, these are popular instruments due to their compact size, relatively low cost and speed of operation. Modern magnetometers can store a huge amount of data (over 2 gigabytes per hectare) thanks to advancements in computer processing. The latest computers allow for more efficient downloading, handling and display of data, greatly increasing the speed at which surveys can be processed and the results interpreted. During a survey, readings are normally taken every 25 centimetres (10 in)

ABOVE: *Graeme Attwood using geophysics at Brancaster.*

along lines a metre apart, then downloaded to a computer for processing. The grid squares are stitched together to display an image showing the patterns of magnetism within the survey area.

When conducting a magnetometry survey, archaeologists must be careful to avoid magnetic contamination from items such as zips, jewellery or credit cards. The presence of a vehicle can affect instruments up to 20 metres (66 ft) away – which restricts their use in urban areas, but helps when looking for something like a lost aeroplane in a greenfield location.

Magnetometers can normally detect down to depths of 2 metres (6½ ft). However, the technique will only work when past activity has produced a measurable amount of magnetic contrast. Therefore graves will rarely show up, because it is normally the case that the same soil will be put back in the hole very quickly after being dug up, and bones are not magnetic! At the Northwood site, magnetometry helped to identify the extent of the building, which could then be better defined using radar.

John Gater

that many of the nearby buildings had benefited from material from Northwood. It was extraordinary that the two columns had survived.

One of the key questions we hoped to answer was whether or not Northwood was a grand palace built in the same style as Hampton Court. This kind of question makes me a little uneasy, as it can be hard to answer from the limited number of finds we might unearth in three days. Even if we uncover a few high-status items, this can't be assumed to determine the overall appearance of the building.

With Jackie McKinley leading the archaeology, we had an experienced *Time Team* expert on hand to make the key decisions. By 11 o'clock the first trench was ready to go in, based on John's initial mag survey.

Phil would be placing a trench near to Martin's initial excavations from forty years ago, where he had discovered the base of a tower on the east side of the gate. We would be looking to see if we could find the tower on the other side. Martin had brought along a list of all his previous finds, including bricks, glass and pottery. Tudor bricks are fairly distinctive. He was particularly keen on a piece of glass from around 1525 which has a fragment of Wolsey's motto, 'God is my Helper', etched on the surface.

We had also enlisted the help of historian Suzannah Lipscomb, an expert on the Tudor period, and Kent Rawlinson, who would be able to guide us through the complexities of Tudor architecture. Suzannah had already managed to track down a reference that proved to be the

RIGHT: *A sample of stained glass, possibly from the windows of the Great Hall.*

OPPOSITE PAGE: *Phil starting the trench over the gatehouse area. We were hoping to find evidence of towers on either side.*

HOW TO USE HISTORICAL RECORDS

On every *Time Team* dig, before the first trench is opened, many weeks have been spent assessing, researching and visiting the site. From this pre-excavation work a project design is created, describing both why the archaeology is being conducted and what questions the work hopes to answer. This allows the site director to target their resources. Pre-excavation techniques such as researching primary historical documents and where to locate previous archaeological reports are therefore essential.

Archival research is often the first step. Primary historical documents such as land and tax records, maps, photographs, deeds, wills, parish records, diaries, letters and newspapers are all excellent places to start. At Northwood, primary evidence included a plan of the site showing various stages of construction during the 1520s, and a reference to the grandeur of the palace made by the French ambassador in 1527. Locating documents such as these often begins in a public or university library or an online archive search. The National Archives in Kew, London, is the UK government's official archive, containing a huge variety of records covering over 1,000 years of history, from paper scrolls and parchments through to digital files and archived websites. English Heritage also has a huge collection of photographs, drawings, reports and publications relating to England's archaeology. Almost every county and most cities will have their own records office, containing historical documents relating to the area. Some private collections of

historical documents also exist, particularly when a large estate has remained in the hands of one family for many generations. Always talk to locals when researching a site, as they may be able to provide access to private collections of documents or share oral history about the area.

Archaeologists will also search for any previous site reports prepared by others who have excavated the site. Northwood had been previously excavated by Professor Martin Biddle in the 1950s, and his reports were immensely important in guiding the project; this highlights the importance of properly recording excavations for the future. Reports like these can be sourced through your local Historic Environment Record (HER), formerly known as the Sites and Monuments Record (SMR). These records are largely available online and are kept and updated by county or district councils. It is also worth checking local commercial archaeological units for any reports relating to the site that have not been transferred onto the HER.

ABOVE: *Poring over old historical documents, an essential task before any excavation.*

origin of the high opinion of Northwood's status. In 1527 the French ambassador to England, Du Bellay, visited Catherine when she was housed at Northwood. We may have to allow for a bit of flattery here, but he referred to the 'sumptious buildings' with 'goodly galleries all gilt above' and other 'gorgeous devices'.

At that time in Europe there was a great deal of sympathy for the queen, particularly because of her Catholic faith and the poor treatment she received at the hands of Henry. The general feeling was that she had done little to deserve her fate, and that she had been cast out as a result of Henry's infatuation with Anne Boleyn. It seems ironic that it would be Wolsey's failure to serve his master's desires in this matter that would eventually lead to his downfall and execution. Wolsey did little to ease Catherine's isolation at Northwood.

Kent had with him a copy of a survey made for Henry that provided a plan of the site. It was clear that over a ten-year period from 1520 he had built an Outer Court (or Base Court) and Long Gallery. All we had to do was to find them!

As well as the standard geophysics, we had Jimmy's latest bit of radar gear that should help us to find the key features. We hoped his references to 'state-of-the-art images' and promises of 'foundations seen in 3D' would not turn out to be overly optimistic.

Phil's opening trench began to reveal walls at a fairly shallow depth, and there was a lot of distinctive Tudor brick. Along with Martin's previous work, we now had confirmation that we were somewhere in the central axis of the building. This was helpful, as Tudor buildings are often symmetrical.

By 12.30 p.m. on Day One our finds included three pieces of maiolica floor tile, glazed and then hand-painted with an attractive blue and yellow design. Paul was able to identify these as being of Dutch origin, evidence that there had been some

LEFT: *Suzannah Lipscomb, our historian for this shoot, and Professor Martin Biddle brief Victor on his illustration of the gatehouse; see page 188.*

Some of the pieces of floor tile actually fitted together.

RIGHT: *Pottery expert Paul Blinkhorn and Danni Wootton admire the maiolica floor tile.*

ABOVE: *By Day Two Phil's trench had begun to produce a wide range of finds.*

high-status tiling on the floors of the gatehouses. Of rather lower status was a sardine can and a teaspoon, which Martin suggested was left over from the last meal of the previous dig in the 1950s!

Trench 2, opened by Raksha and Matt, was placed on what we hoped would be the dividing point between the chapel and the Great Hall. Towards the end of Day One, a third trench was located over the north-east corner, which according to the geophysics scan might have been the eastern extent of the building. If this turned out to be the case, we would at last have a major dimension of the main structure.

Trench 2 had begun to look like a cellar by the last hour of the day, containing all the debris from the building's destruction.

ABOVE: *Close-up of maiolica tile, possibly imported from Italy.*

At the start of Day Two Phil decided to extend his trench to see if he could locate the moat that we knew had surrounded the site. He was already finding a range of medieval English and French pottery.

IN MATT AND Raksha's trench the cellar was getting deeper, and they were finding fragments of decorated wall plaster. Digging trenches through demolition rubble is hard work and requires keeping a sharp eye open for any fragments of original intact stonework.

Towards the end of Day Two, it was decided to investigate anomalies that might represent the Base Court. If this feature existed and was on the scale that Martin and Kent were expecting, it would increase the likelihood of this palace being on the same grand scale as Hampton Court. Kent had been able to show us images of Oxmoor Castle, a building with a huge gate tower, slightly more modest than Hampton Court but of the

BELOW: *Floor tiles from the Great Hall, confirming the existence of a high-status building.*

LEFT: *In Raksha's trench there was a considerable depth of deposits, perhaps an indication of a cellar.*

right period. It suggested how impressive the approach to Northwood might have been.

Phil had been able to uncover more of the moat that would have surrounded the main building, and at the end of Day Two we at last began to find more evidence of high-status decoration. Kent pointed out that the towers at the main entrance to the palace would have been 15 metres high, with three layers of decoration and probably a huge coat of arms.

In Tracey's trench she had uncovered fragments of richly decorated glass that would have been part of the east window of the chapel.

More fragments of floor tile.

This chapel had been the site of one of the major events of European history when Cardinal Wolsey brought Henry together with some of the leaders of Europe, including the French king's representative and from England the Duke of Norfolk and Sir Thomas More, to sign the Treaty of the More, which helped to ensure peace between England and France for the following decade. Suzannah was able to refer to a contemporary document that dated the meeting precisely to 30 August 1525. Henry, in return for a substantial pension, agreed not to attack French interests, and the treaty was given religious affirmation by a swearing-in ceremony in the chapel. It was nice to think that as the statesmen stood in the chapel making history, they would

have seen the light passing through the beautiful glass, fragments of which Tracey now held in her hand. Glass often turns up on these kinds of sites and the conservation of it is important, as it laminates very easily.

By the end of Day Two, we were no nearer to finding the Base Court, and a trench dug by Cassie along one possible axis had failed to find any trace of walls. John and Jimmy were going to have to spread their search wider. Had we underestimated the scale of the palace?

OPPOSITE PAGE: *Towards the end of Day Two we were able to see clearly the brick base of a large tower on one side of the gateway.*

BELOW: *Danni, Tony and Paul surveying the day's finds.*

HOW TO RECORD A TRENCH

Recording is absolutely essential on any archaeological site. If you do not record everything, then the physical effort of digging the trench and cleaning the archaeology goes to waste. There is only one opportunity to get it right: once a trench has been dug, the archaeology has often been destroyed, therefore producing a detailed and accurate record is one of the most important things an archaeologist can do.

There are three key stages in the recording of a site. First, during the actual excavation process, we continually record the archaeological features and deposits as we excavate them; this vital stage makes it possible for us to analyse the site's chronology later on. Second, once the trench has reached a key stage in the excavation or has been completely finished, we plan and photograph both the trench and the archaeology within it, draw sections of the deposits, record the exact location and produce written context records. Finally, after the excavation is finished, all the information collected is brought back to the offices along with the finds to be processed and investigated further as we prepare the excavation report.

From the opening of the very first trench a context list is started: this list records all of the deposits across the site and allows us to assign to each individual deposit its own unique context number. These contexts are the building blocks we use to put together a picture of how the site has developed over time. Therefore, the earliest context number will be for the natural geology. Then, as features are constructed, ditches are dug, walls are built and floors are

ABOVE: *A trench prepared for recording at Northwood. Note the ranging rods and the sharpness of the trench edges.*

laid down and so on, we are able to track this chronological development and build up the stratigraphic matrix of the site to understand how the archaeology has changed.

Once a trench has reached a key stage or has been finished completely, it is then essential to photograph and plan the archaeology. So after Phil, Raksha, Matt, Tracey or one of the other on-site archaeologists has finished cleaning the trench, it will be photographed. When photographing, archaeologists always use photographic scales: these are poles usually 1 or 2 metres (3 or 6½ ft) long and divided into 10-centimetre (4 in) or 50-centimetre (20 in) sections alternately painted red and white. The scales help provide an idea of the size of the trench and the archaeology within it. Being up high is the best angle from which to take a photograph of an entire trench, as it allows us to see the archaeology in plan and how different features relate to each other.

The next step is to start planning the trench.

This involves climbing down into the trench – much to the annoyance of those who have just spent hours carefully cleaning it up. A pin is banged into either end of the trench and then these pins are surveyed in using the GPS equipment to give us the exact location, which is plotted onto a site plan. Recording the exact location of trenches is essential work so that if anyone wishes to conduct further work on the site in the future they can easily find out where *Time Team* dug their trenches. Older sites, such as the antiquarian sites in the nineteenth century or even sites dug in the 1950s, can cause problems, as it is often very hard to calculate the exact position of their trenches because they did not have access to the state-of-the-art technology that we use today.

Once the surveying is completed, a long tape measure is laid out between the two pins. This tape measure is then used as a base line in order to plan the trench. A second smaller tape is used to do offsets (measuring from the base line), allowing for the limits of the trench to be planned as well as any features within the trench. All this information is hand-drawn onto a plan. For more intricate areas that require detailed planning, a planning frame is used. This is normally a metre square made out of wood or metal that is divided up into smaller 20-centimetre (8 in) squares. This can then be placed over an area within the trench to act as a visual aid, in order to plan the archaeology with a high degree of accuracy. When planning a trench there is a real mix of both old-fashioned drawing by hand and state-of-the-art surveying technology, providing both clarity and accuracy. Upon completion of the planning, all the details of the trench can be seen on one drawing and this can provide a good indication of which areas may need further investigation. Sondages (a small exploratory test hole) are often used against walls, perhaps to find a floor surface or sometimes in the corner of a finished trench to check there is no more archaeology below the excavated layers.

Once the trench has been planned and any sections drawn (we draw at least one 'representative section' as an example of the deposits which seal the archaeology), the context records are written. A record is produced for each unique context number assigned (for example for walls, floors, the fills of ditches, the overlying deposits and so on) to describe that particular archaeological deposit or feature in detail. So for example, for a wall we record the dimensions, what it's built from (stone, brick etc.), the type of mortar (sandy, ashy etc.) and how the wall relates stratigraphically to other features or deposits. This is often the most time-consuming part of all excavations, which is why on *Time Team* we get a Day 4 to finish the recording.

Steve Thompson, Wessex Archaeology

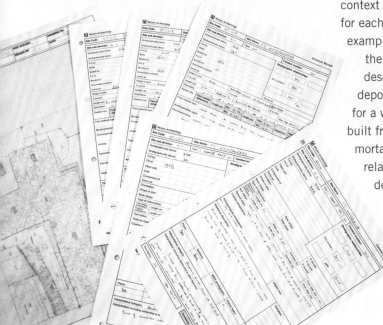

LEFT: *A typical set of records for a trench.*

On Day Three we began to search for evidence of the Long Gallery. Trenches 5 and 6 were placed across the line of the gallery.

KENT RAWLINSON WAS able to refer to documents that described the gallery as being over 253 feet (77 metres) in length, as measured in Henry's day. The search was hampered by the need to navigate around the school tennis courts and the area of woodland covering the only place we could excavate.

Jimmy's final radar scans had produced some 'linears', which is as vague as it sounds, and neither he nor John felt optimistic. Jackie felt it was worth one last try. The situation was not helped by the final trench being the subject of a five-pound wager as to whether we would find a pipe, conduit or wall. With a few hours left, the final throw of the dice was taken.

Back in Tracey's trench we were at last finding substantial walls, which enabled us to imagine the size of the structure that would have originally stood above them. It was clearly an important find. As with all *Time Team* trenches, we needed the findings accurately recorded for the final report, especially considering the scheduled status of the site. Wessex Archaeology were on hand, and I wanted to get their view of the Northwood recording process. Steve Thompson is a veteran of numerous *Time Teams* and his experience is invaluable at our digs; in the mini skills masterclass on page 184 he explains how to record a trench.

Phil's trench at last revealed the octagonal shape of the original towers. Combined with Martin's work, this had added to our

ABOVE: *Many of the building remains were at a relatively shallow depth, beneath the surface of the school playing fields.*

understanding of Northwood, but we all felt a bit frustrated. Sites like Northwood are often frustrating for us, because the potential goal – to find a palace as imposing as Hampton Court – can be difficult to live up to on a location where material has been removed and there has been considerable demolition.

One of the distinctive aspects of Henry's attitude to buildings he no longer required was his determination to virtually wipe them out and sell every last brick to the highest bidder. It might even be that this 'slighting', as it's referred to elsewhere, was particularly thorough in cases where a building was associated with a person who had fallen out of favour.

In discussions after the shoot Martin and I discussed the possible location of the palace: both he and Kent felt that we might have underestimated its size and had been looking too close to the interior. I hope that in the next year I might be able to persuade John to return and extend his search.

However, we did find considerable remains of wall foundations in Tracey's trench, and the geophysics results enabled us to locate the main gatehouse and the dimensions of the main palace building. Victor was able to produce another of his marvellous illustrations to remind us of the moment when Catherine stood at the gates of Northwood, surrounded by her retinue of servants and soldiers and perhaps admiring the beautiful columns.

ABOVE: *Jimmy's Tudor drain! Not quite the Outer Court wall we had been hoping for, but an unexpected surprise.*

Northwood reminded me of another Tudor palace we had excavated at Richmond in series 5. In one particularly deep trench we had searched for the walls of a palace that had been the final lodging of Elizabeth I and the place where she would die. We found many pieces of amazing architectural fragments, but in one main trench all we found were the beer mugs and pipe stems of the demolition crew!

TOP RIGHT: *A document presented to the school at the end of Day Three, bearing replica seals.*

BELOW: *Victor's illustration of Catherine of Aragon arriving at Northwood.*

VIEW FROM THE TRENCHES

TRACEY

As a field archaeologist, the prospect of excavating a site that has already been investigated always leads to mixed feelings. On the one hand, you have a pretty good idea of what to expect, so the sense of anticipation and discovery is not as great as on an unknown site. On the other hand, you know there will be archaeology below the ground and so there is the chance to add to the knowledge from earlier work, gaining a better understanding of the site as a whole.

Northwood was one such site: as it had been partially investigated in the 1950s, we already had a reasonable idea of what we would find once we opened the trenches, and I will admit to some mixed feelings about what we might discover during our own excavations. However, the trench that we opened and which I worked in over the three days proved to be a good illustration of how additional evaluation can add to the overall picture of a site. Once we had removed the demolition levels down to the top of the surviving archaeology, exposing the series of walls we had been expecting to find from the earlier research, we also discovered a rough chalk wall that had not been previously excavated and which had also not shown up in the geophysics due to the nature of the background demolition deposits. This wall turned out to be one of the earliest on the site, and, along with the fragments of painted window glass that I excavated in a small section through some earlier demolition, this added further detail to the story of the construction and subsequent rebuilding of the Manor of the Moor.

Nothing can bring a site to life as much as finds like the decorated glass, which made a lovely end to the trench on Day Three. It was also good to beat geophysics to a wall for a change!

ABOVE: *Tracey discussing the details of her trench with Richard K. Morris.*

BELTON PARK

Belton Camp in Lincolnshire was a place that changed the way wars were fought forever.

THOUSANDS OF MEN lived temporarily at the site as part of their intensive training to use the most advanced weapon of the First World War – the machine gun. The camp was erected at great speed and many of the soldiers passed through it in just six short weeks.

From Mesolithic hunters and nomadic herdsmen to more modern examples like refugee camps or protest settlements, the examination of how much or how little evidence is left behind by a temporary camp has been an important thread in archaeological research. It makes us face the fact that even when we know from relatively recent records that a site has been occupied, it can often be difficult to find any evidence of this. It makes us realize how much more difficult it would be to uncover traces of prehistoric activity.

It's clear that certain kinds of human activity can leave relatively little trace. This can make us more aware of the importance of features like rubbish pits, or the faint traces left by the beam slots of wooden buildings. In some cases, the mark left by water dripping from a roof may be the only evidence that a structure once existed.

We knew that over 130,000 men had passed through Belton Camp, and we had photographs of the exterior and interior of the buildings and army records of the activities on the site. We also

RIGHT: *The grand house at Belton, where thousands of men were encamped during the First World War. The main house was built by the Brownlow family in the seventeenth century.*

had plans of where the main barrack rooms, cookhouse and other features had existed. The main question was going to be: exactly what was left of the camp?

Tony's opening piece to camera set the key goals.

TONY'S PIECE TO CAMERA

" *We are at the magnificent Belton House in Lincolnshire, but for once we are not here to find a missing wing or to dig up the extensive ornamental gardens.*

Almost a century ago, there was another community in residence, and they weren't servants of the Brownlow family who owned the estate.

For years the army camped on the Brownlows' property. There were thousands of them, and in the First World War one of the main reasons they came here was to learn how to use machine guns.

We want to turn the clock back a century and find out just what happened when Belton went to war. "

The Belton Park Machine Gun Training Camp was the first of its kind in Britain and is a very important part of the history of British warfare. Although we had a set of plans, we wanted to find out how accurate they were and how the site had developed over its lifespan. Under National Trust ownership the site had been well protected:

RIGHT: *Photographs of the barrack blocks where the men lived provided us with useful pictorial evidence.*

no ploughing had taken place there in the recent past. It was possible that there would be a good level of preservation, although the records showed that the site was cleared after the camp was decommissioned around 1920, allowing the Brownlow family to return the area to private parkland.

As usual, the project design set out our aims for the shoot.

Research aim 1: How did the site develop over its lifespan and how is this reflected in existing plans?

Research aim 2: What is the condition and archaeological potential of surviving subsurface archaeological remains?

Research aim 3: What is the character and potential function of the structure at the south-east edge of the site?

Research aim 4: What can be determined in regard to the post-military life of the camp – did the site continue to be used?

On Day One Phil opened up a trench at the point identified on the plan as the YMCA. This was one of the key social sites of the camp and one of the few places where all the ranks would have socialized together. An organization known as NAAFI (Navy, Army and Air Force Institutes) was responsible for providing recreation on military bases, including shops, canteens and clubs.

Matt and Raksha opened Trench 2 over

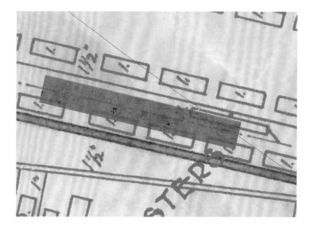

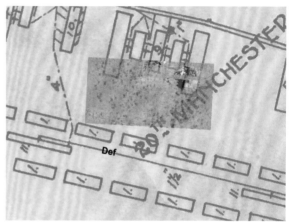

ABOVE: *The first set of rather inconclusive geophysics results laid over the potential kitchen area. On either side are the rows of barrack blocks.*

what we hoped would be the cookhouse building, and Trench 3 was placed over what we hoped would be a barrack block. The limited geophysics results from John and his team posed an immediate problem: although we knew exactly where the barrack blocks were, they were throwing up very little evidence on the geophysics.

However, the archaeology in Trench 1 was more encouraging. It became clear that the YMCA was the site of a wide range of artefacts left behind once the camp had closed. By the

USING A MINI DIGGER

On a *Time Team* dig, our first step is to check for any services within the dig area. Then the project design is consulted for notes on the soil type or the type of archaeology we are expecting to uncover. If we are expecting to find burials, for example, the machine will be operated at a slower pace. Working in fields is always a bit easier than digging up someone's manicured lawn. We lay down plywood or polythene to protect a lawn and put the excavated soil on top. When the turf is removed, we try to keep it intact so that once it is laid back down it has a big enough root bed to carry on growing. Next we take the topsoil off, which is invariably a different colour to the subsoil. The topsoil and subsoil must be kept separate, partly for the sake of the archaeology, but also because this makes reinstating the trench easier, as turf regrows a lot faster from topsoil.

We always go down in very small layers of about 2 or 3 millimetres. Removing very fine layers allows us to identify archaeology and also makes backfilling much quicker, as it is easier to compact very fine soil. As we get nearer to the archaeological level we tend to use the bucket more like a mechanical scraper than a digger. Once we definitely hit archaeology, the rest is then done by hand. An experienced driver will usually be able to feel any solid bits of stone, such as a Roman wall, through the excavator, and can often see features like post holes and ditch marks in the soil from above.

When we backfill, we always put the subsoil in first, in layers of about 10 centimetres (4 in), then compact it with the bucket. It is very important not to beat the soil down, or you will end up with a shortage of soil. Next the topsoil goes back in, and a piece of plywood is used to compact the topsoil. Finally we re-turf; the last piece of turf removed is the first piece of turf back into the trench. If these guidelines are followed, there shouldn't be any shortage of soil or lots of soil left over. It should be impossible to see where the trench was.

Ian Barclay

LEFT: *Ian Barclay and his 'assistant' Kerry Ely. In his spare time Kerry is also in charge of Time Team's logistics!*

ABOVE: *A selection of finds from the NAAFI trench.*

middle of the afternoon, we had found pieces of a
pot bearing a War Office stamp and a date of 1915,
some beer bottles and, towards the end of the day,
a fragment of a Horlicks pot with the YMCA logo
on it.

All the trenches produced fairly large amounts of
pottery. By the end of Day Three, we were able to
look at a quantity of white china shards, particularly
from the YMCA and cookhouse area. At Belton,
many of the pottery items had transfer-printed
designs on them. In particular, it was interesting to
see the logo of the Machine Gun Corps on some
items. This crockery must have been purchased by
the Ministry of Defence in vast amounts, probably
from potteries in the Staffordshire area; it was a
fascinating detail to see the crossed-machine-gun
logo on the items we found.

*Close-up of a remnant of a tea mug
bearing the YMCA stamp.*

INDUSTRIAL POTTERY

In the eighteenth and nineteenth centuries the industrial revolution brought about huge changes in the pottery industry. Vast improvements in infrastructure, such as roads, canals and railways, opened up new markets by allowing for larger volumes of goods to be transported over longer distances. Canals in particular were a major factor in the success of the pottery industry, as the waterways provided the perfect mode of transportation for fragile products.

Another key development was the rise in the use of moulds, for the first time since the Roman period. Around the mid-eighteenth century, moulds would have been made from either biscuit form (unglazed but fired clay) or plaster of Paris. The use of moulds not only made it possible to produce ceramics of elaborate shapes and designs, such as teapots in the forms of

pineapples or cauliflowers, but more importantly allowed manufacturers to rapidly churn out high volumes of identical vessels. By the end of the nineteenth century, plates were being produced in their millions. The effects of this manufacturing boom caused the price of ceramics to drop, meaning that items that were previously prohibitively expensive became available to a larger proportion of the population. Even working-class families were able to buy good-quality ceramics.

As production increased, so did the size of the kilns. Large bottle kilns became a dominant feature of the landscape, particularly at the heart of the British ceramic industry around Staffordshire. These larger kilns needed increased heat regulation in order to ensure that the wares were fired correctly, without undue losses. In order to modernize this process, Josiah Wedgwood developed his system of pyrometric

ABOVE: *A porcelain dish made during the Wan Li dynasty and imported from China (left), alongside an imitation porcelain dish made in Bristol during the 1660s.*

beads: small balls of ceramic material were added to the kiln, and these would indicate by changing colour that the desired temperature had been reached.

Most of the ceramics being mass produced within these kilns would have been influenced by imports from the Far East, such as Chinese porcelain. Imported porcelain proved to be incredibly popular during the early industrial period, largely because it was seen to be exotic and only attainable by those with wealth and power. Prior to the eighteenth century, the secret to making porcelain remained unknown within Europe, and many attempts were made to replicate the product, with varying degrees of success. Early imitations used a soft paste, which was achieved by mixing white clay with a variety of materials, including ground glass (also known as frit) or steatite. In 1741, after much research, William Cookworthy discovered kaolin (also known as china clay or Cornish stone), allowing for the manufacture of porcelain-quality products on British soil for the first time.

Cream-coloured earthenware (known as creamware) was also discovered and mass produced during the second half of the eighteenth century as a rival to porcelain. The invention of creamware has been attributed to Thomas Whieldon of Staffordshire; however, it is more commonly associated with Josiah Wedgwood, who in 1759 began producing it at his Burslem factory. *Time Team* found many sherds of this iconic creamware when they excavated at Burslem. In the 1760s a factory in Leeds began experimenting with various types of glaze in order to produce a rival creamware, and eventually an entirely new glaze was created, similar to porcelain, which became known as pearlware.

While porcelain and creamware were generally reserved for the table, earthenwares were still being manufactured for use in kitchens and dairies. These wares were often produced by smaller potteries, which were unable to compete on the industrial scale. Most of the earthenwares had a hard, red fabric, as they were fired in an oxidizing kiln, and were often finished with a yellowish lead glaze, although local variations did occur.

ABOVE *A sherd of creamware found on a* Time Team *dig at Burslem.*

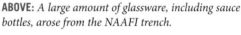

ABOVE: *A large amount of glassware, including sauce bottles, arose from the NAAFI trench.*

Pottery finds bearing the logo of the Machine Gun Corps.

Much of the pottery we found at Belton would be described by experts as 'industrial'. The potteries of the Staffordshire area in the Midlands produced vast quantities of this material, and it can be incredibly useful in identifying and dating sites. Many of the potteries have their own pattern books, which contain specific references to orders from families or organizations for individual pieces of particular designs. We have come across this pottery on virtually every site that we have excavated. One of the most memorable locations was on Nevis in the Caribbean, where deep in the jungle we found dinner services that would have been ordered by the plantation owners in the late eighteenth century. One of our most significant finds of this nature was at a pottery in Staffordshire called Burslem, where in 1999 we unearthed huge caches of this material close to the kilns that would have created it.

In Matt's trench we appeared to have lines of pipe, but very little evidence of the foundations of what should have been one of the more substantial buildings on the site. In Trench 3, over the barrack block, we had found very little at all by the end of Day One.

Belton House had a fascinating history before it became a training camp. The main house was built by the Brownlow family between 1685 and 1688. The Brownlows eventually became earls, and it was the third Earl Brownlow who offered his house to help the war effort. Around 500 huts

were built and the men were put through a brief six-week training regime as part of a brand-new section of the army called the Machine Gun Corps.

The main purpose of the new corps was to create a specialist force to redress the imbalance between the machine-gun strength of the German and British armies. When war broke out in August 1914, the Germans had 12,000 Maxim machine guns and would eventually have over 100,000, in contrast to the British and French, who had under 1,800 machine guns when the war began. The Germans were also better trained. With the potential fire power to kill at a

BELOW: *Vast amounts of creamware scattered the trenches in the NAAFI area.*

LEFT: *A view of the barrack blocks from the surrounding hills.*

distance of over 2 miles and a firing rate of over 200 rounds per minute, the machine gun was the start of the industrialization of death.

The new Machine Gun Corps soon had access to the Vickers machine gun, a rival to the Maxim, and camps like Belton were designed to train up gunners as quickly as possible. There would be more than 80,000 soldiers at Belton at a time. The training involved testing the machine guns for continuous fire, which meant that in a twelve-hour period over a million rounds would be fired without stopping. The Vickers machine gun would become one of the world's deadliest weapons; it was still in use during the Second World War.

RIGHT: *The Vickers machine gun, the lethal weapon used by the Machine Gun Corps.*

Phil's trench was continuing to reveal interesting finds. It also seemed possible that the shape of the building could be determined by locating the path that had run around the outside.

ABOVE: *Phil holding the top of an army swagger stick.*

TRENCH 2 WAS closed down, and Matt and Raksha set off in search of another cookhouse, which appeared to give a strong signal on the geophysics. In Trench 3 Cassie had found a bullet with cordite still in it, but progress was hampered by the care needed to handle the asbestos that was appearing in the trench. Health and safety issues on sites like this can be critical: an important part of each excavation is a health and safety risk assessment, which can often turn out to be longer than the script of the film itself!

Stewart had been gradually going through all the photographic archives of the camp, and on the afternoon of Day Two he made an important observation. By closely examining the footings in one of the photographs, he was able to detect that the huts appeared to be resting on brick or stone plinths, which raised them above the ground – this clearly explained the lack of any responses from the geophysics. In Phil's trench we continued to find more evidence of NAAFI activity, including a cap badge, buttons, a bowl and a buckle. This corresponded with a fascinating find from Day One: this was gently cleaned to reveal the top of a swagger stick, something that would have been carried by many of the soldiers at the camp. Our military expert Martin Brown, archaeological advisor to the Ministry of Defence, was able to point out that the purpose of the swagger stick was to deter soldiers from walking around with their hands in their pockets.

Stewart had by now left the incident room and was heading for the nearby golf course. With so

ABOVE: *Finds from the Machine Gun Corps archive.*

many rounds having been fired at the training camp, he wanted to find the potential target area. There appeared to be a bank near the centre of the golf course, which he was keen to investigate.

We had arranged that on the final day we would actually fire a Vickers machine gun. The process of setting one up gave us a good idea of the weight of the whole unit: the gun itself weighs more than 11 kilograms (25 lb), with a tripod of 18 to 22 kilograms (40 to 50 lb). Once the Vickers was set up, the gunners would become a major target for the Germans. For many gunners life was brutally short. The gunners at Belton referred to themselves as the Suicide Club, and some of them adopted a skull and crossbones as their emblem.

ABOVE: *A Vickers machine gun belt and a Machine Gun Corps badge.*

After giving out a suitable warning to the golfers, we fired the machine gun, and for the first time in nearly a hundred years the sound of the Vickers echoed across the estate.

ABOVE: *Phil getting to grips with the workings of the machine gun. The tank in the foreground supplies water to act as a coolant.*

USING AERIAL PHOTOGRAPHS

Aerial photographs are invaluable to archaeologists as a way of mapping and recording archaeological sites. Sites may be visible in aerial photographs as earthworks, soil, crop or patch marks, many of which are too large, faint or discontinuous to be appreciated at ground level. Hundreds of previously unknown archaeological sites are discovered in this way each year.

One of the first archaeological sites to be documented through aerial archaeology was Stonehenge, photographed by Lieutenant Philip Henry Sharpe in 1906 from a balloon. During the First World War, aerial reconnaissance was undertaken using open-seated biplanes to meet the needs of the military intelligence. O. G. S. Crawford, an observer in the Royal Flying Corps, was one of the first people to recognize the huge potential of large-scale aerial reconnaissance for archaeological purposes. In 1924 he undertook an aerial survey of archaeological sites in Dorset, Hampshire and Wiltshire, publishing the results in his ground-breaking book *Wessex from the Air*.

Today, systematic archaeological aerial surveys document almost the entirety of the UK. There are two types of aerial photograph: vertical and oblique. Vertical photographs are taken looking straight down, providing a plan view. Generally they are captured using machine cameras mounted underneath aeroplanes flying at a high altitude (above 300 metres). Vertical photographs are taken at set intervals so that each frame overlaps slightly with the next, producing blanket coverage across the landscape. Oblique photos are generally taken of an archaeological subject after it has been identified. They are taken closer to the ground, at an angle to the site, using a handheld zoom camera. *Time Team* mostly uses helicopters as an alternative to aeroplanes, as they can hover in mid-air and are easily manoeuvrable.

In 1965, the Royal Commission on the Historic Monuments of England established an Air Photographs Unit, which was taken over by English Heritage in 1999. It is the largest collection in the country, with over two million vertical photographs, largely taken by the RAF or Ordnance Survey, alongside over half a million oblique photographs.

BELOW: *An aerial photograph of Stonehenge taken in 1906 from a balloon.*

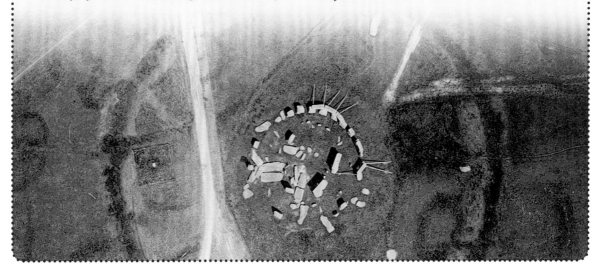

On Day Three we closed down Cassie's trench and concentrated on Trench 5, where Matt and Raksha were finding some evidence of what may have been a cookhouse.

FRANCIS PRYOR, WHO was leading the excavation, kept the momentum going despite the frustration we all felt at the apparent lack of evidence. Trench 1 still continued to produce finds, however, and it was fascinating to be able to see some of the photographs of the camp's interiors.

Archive photography was of great importance at the Belton site. It was used particularly by Stewart to locate possible excavation sites within the camp and in the surrounding countryside. Stewart has often used photographs to locate specific features: this involves trying to distinguish elements of the current landscape in spite of changes in tree cover and the development of modern buildings.

The archive photographs also gave us the chance to see the faces of those people who had occupied the barracks. We were joined by two families whose grandfathers had taken part in First World War battles: it was a poignant reminder of the human cost of war and provided

BELOW: *A trench across the barrack-block area from the air.*

ABOVE: *One of the soldiers from the Machine Gun Corps.*

the kind of oral history that is often absent from other archaeological sites. Rosemary and David Musson had been able to visit the memorial in the church in Grantham that commemorated their uncle, Lieutenant Graham Musson, who joined the Lincolnshire Yeomanry and was trained at Belton. As was often the case, machine gunners at the front were called upon to cover the retreat of their comrades, and after just such an action Graham Musson was shot as he returned from his machine-gun post to rejoin the lines. To be able to show a picture of him during the programme was very moving. Phil Harding was particularly interested in these stories, as he had family members who had fought during the First World War.

Stewart's accumulation of a large number of documentary archive photographs, reminded me of other *Time Team*s on which we have been able to use this sort of information to help guide the archaeology. We had filmed the excavation of a B-17 bomber at Reedham Marshes in Norfolk for an episode broadcast in 1999; it was Stewart's use of the detailed documents describing the structure of the plane and the stories of the crew from the squadron who had survived that enabled us to find precise information during the excavations. See the mini skills masterclass on page 208 to find out more about how archaeologists use historical photographs in their work.

Doing this kind of archaeology on sites connected to people who have died during warfare has always made a difference to how the team operate and to the general atmosphere on the site. Excavations on sites like the Spitfire at Wierre-Effroy in France for the programme shown in 2000 made all of us realize exactly what kind of sacrifices had been made in the past by people who went to war.

On the final day, we were able to visit a hut that had been moved from Belton – possibly the only structure to survive from the camp. It now

ABOVE: *A surviving barrack block nearby, now used as the village hall.*

USING HISTORICAL PHOTOGRAPHS

Historical photographs are a hugely important and useful resource for archaeologists. The photographs of the Belton site provided the solution when we could not work out why the huts weren't appearing on the geophysics. They also gave us a picture of the now lost interiors of the huts, as well as a connection to the people who once used and occupied the site.

When researching a site, there are a number of key places where you can search for copies, or even originals, of historical photographs relating to your site of interest. The first place to look is on the internet. Many online sites deal with old photographs; some are hosted by local authorities, communities or interest groups, others by professional photographic companies wishing to advertise their products. District archives, city records offices and local studies libraries will all generally have holdings of old photographs which are available to be searched through by the public. It is also worth looking in local bookshops, many of which will stock published volumes of local historical photographs.

Occasionally, it is also possible to track down the original photograph itself within private collections. Members of the local community are often a wealth of information, especially when it comes to historical photographs. Old photos form an immediate link between the past and present, and looking through them with local residents is a great opportunity to do some oral history work as people reminisce about old times. Make sure you keep a register of any photographs that have been loaned to you, to avoid possible misunderstandings later on. Also,

ABOVE: *Cassie and Rob examining historical photographs of the Belton site.*

if you intend to use an image in a publicly accessible form, such as a presentation or part of a display, make sure you have permission from the owner of the photograph and always acknowledge the source (or sources) of the image.

When archaeologists study historical photographs, there are a number of important questions to consider, such as when was the photograph taken? Where was it taken? Who took it and why? What is the subject of the photo and what are the details in the background? Occasionally, the answers to these questions will be obvious; when they are not, attempting to find the answers can open up entirely new and extremely interesting avenues of research.

When studying historical photographs, it is vitally important to bear in mind the historical significance attached to photography. The cost of owning a camera and maintaining a dark room would have been out of the reach of the majority of people in the nineteenth and early twentieth century. It wasn't until the mid-twentieth century, with the development of cameras such as the Box Brownie, that photography became available to the general public. The early technology was also bulky. Films needed long exposure times and developing them was a complex process. This meant that early photographs could not show anything moving quickly. As a result, the majority of shots were of landscapes or posed portraits, rarely showing depictions of everyday life. They instead aimed to present everything in the best possible light, which is why many early photographs look so very serious and restrained, in a similar manner to the Victorian and Edwardian oil paintings.

Just like other archaeological artefacts, old photographs decay over time. They need to be handled carefully and correctly cared for. When looking through historical photographs, wear gloves if possible and only ever hold the photograph at its edges. It is best to store photographs out of the light in a stable, acid-free environment. Keeping photographs in individual polyester film envelopes is a good idea; this also allows them to be handled without contaminating the surface of the print. Lastly, avoid marking the photo. However, if this needs to be done, use a soft pencil and write lightly on the back of the photograph.

BELOW: *Historical photograph showing a view over the Belton camp.*

ABOVE: *Victor's illustration of soldiers going over the top to face enemy machine guns.*

serves as Denton's village hall, so Cassie and Martin Brown were able to take a good look around. Martin's photographs from the archive show a typical hut interior; as he memorably said, one could imagine the smell of 'wet soldiers, Woodbines and machine-gun oil'.

Ironically, on the final day we did find some more pottery evidence, but it turned out to be prehistoric!

Stewart's search of the golf course eventually came up trumps: he and Phil returned with handfuls of lead bullets, which would have been fired from the centre of the Belton range nearly 600 yards away. The weight of them was a sober reminder of the killing power of the machine gun and of just how brave soldiers must have been at the start of the war to climb out of their trenches and face a stream of such bullets coming from

the German lines. At the battle of Ypres in October 1914, the British expeditionary force numbered over 165,000 men: of these, over 75,000 died, largely decimated by German machine guns.

Over the three days at Belton, we had seen how vital original documents and photographs were to our strategy, as was the presence of military experts like Martin Brown and Andy Robertshaw. We had also been able to talk to families whose grandfathers had fought in the wars. The team had added its contribution to the story of the Machine Gun Corps, who after their training days at Belton would go on to fight in every major theatre of war over the next decades.

Of the 170,000 men who were trained here, it is worth remembering that many were young men barely over eighteen years of age who had grown up on farms. More than a third never returned. Knowledge of this made the finds from the NAAFI hut even more poignant: a memory of a time of pleasure and light-heartedness before a trip to the front.

LEFT: *The interior of the NAAFI: a memorably atmospheric picture.*

Y.M.C.A. No. 3. Keighley Hut, Belton Park.

CASSIE

A historical plan of the site showed that a row of huts had once stood beside the main road. This seemed like a nice easy target, so we opened up a trench alongside the road, hoping to encounter one of the huts. It was also something of an experiment. By digging a trench which we were almost certain would contain a hut, we would be able to find out the sort of archaeology the huts had left behind. This would then allow us to recognize similar features, if we came across them, when digging other areas of the site.

This turned out to be a good idea, as the archaeology proved to be very ephemeral. One of our major finds was the remains of a beam slot across the front of the hut. It may have looked fairly unimpressive on camera, but while we were digging it was possible to see a really nice dark-brown stripe set within the surrounding orange clay. This brown imprint

BELOW *One of our trenches at Belton, showing how shallow and ephemeral the archaeology was at this site.*

was created by something organic sitting on the soil and decaying. The structures that once stood on site were only in use for around a decade before being pulled down and taken away, so the fact that they left any imprint at all and we were able to find anything is, I think, very impressive. We could have easily found nothing, as the chances of finding the archaeological footprint for a wooden structure without any foundations or post holes is very slim.

Aside from the beam imprints, we also found evidence relating to fire hearths. All of the huts would have had a small fire within them, in order to keep the guys warm. These fires were standing on and were surrounded by asbestos tiles, with fire clay holding it all together. Asbestos tiles are the sort of thing you can't easily reuse. This meant that most of them were left behind, so when we found them we knew where the hearth would have been. Once we had found both the stove at one end and the beam slots at the other, it was very easy to estimate the width of the huts.

Obviously, we had to excavate the huts extremely carefully, partly because of the presence of asbestos, and partly because the remains were so ephemeral. If we had dug quickly, we may have missed them. It became very obvious that most of what was originally there had been recycled. Anything that had any kind of salvageable value had been taken away. The only things left behind were things like asbestos tiles, burnt clay or spent shell casings. It was also noticeably a very clean site; the materials that did remain had been left in nice neat piles before being buried in pits. In a similar manner to archaeological investigations, the army aimed to leave the site the way they found it and so reinstated the picturesque park landscape.

Aside from digging, I also went off with Martin to have a look at a collection of huts that have been turned into the local village hall. This gave us a really good insight into what the interior of the huts may have looked like. You could clearly see where all of the bunks would have been. Standing there made me think of just how many people would have been packed into each hut.

ABOVE: *The* Time Team *diggers striding across Belton Park. Cassie is second from the right.*

WHERE NEXT FOR *TIME TEAM?*

It is a strange feeling to watch something that you have created develop and morph into a different entity. *Time Team* developed its own inner logic as it grew into a much bigger phenomenon – a production juggernaut with its own momentum.

RIGHT: *The team from series three at Templecombe, Somerset.*

AFTER TWENTY YEARS, not surprisingly, the team had expanded considerably. This was partly due to the higher profile that the show had achieved, the goal being to produce a programme for Channel 4 that would sit well in a prime-time slot. On the final day's filming at Brancaster, we had more than seventy-five people on site! The filming was carried out by three camera crews, amounting to twelve people in total, including a jib or crane for camera shots, a helicopter and a fourth unit capturing shots for cutaways.

It is probably stating the obvious that it is just not possible for all these people to easily share the flow or direction of the narrative. In these circumstances the schedule – the list of sequences that need to be shot according to the script – begins to dominate. The exact focus of the main archaeological process where an excavation is attempting to unlock an answer to a key question can get lost. It becomes harder for the producers to make sure that the key camera teams are focused on the most important archaeological discoveries and the strategic thinking leading the team from hour to hour.

The result was that over time the programme began to look more like a documentary, rather than the reality-style show it had been in its earlier days. The immediacy of the viewers' relationship with the archaeology had been to some extent lost, and the team itself had become less spontaneous in their responses.

Not all the changes that have taken place in the last five to seven years have been negative. But the accumulation of an additional managerial and organizational infrastructure had moved our attention away from the core subject of the archaeology. In addition, the expanded production team in turn increased the budget, which began to make *Time Team* look very expensive in relation to the viewing figures it could sustain in a challenging market. *Time Team*'s reality-style approach and its key innovation of 'archaeology in three days' had

been overtaken by many programmes addressing the same themes. Taking into account the *Big Brother* effect and the popularity of formats featuring competition and elimination, the current TV zeitgeist has changed considerably from when we began.

You may be able to guess from the above that I was able to accept Channel 4's recent decision to concentrate on *Time Team* documentaries, rather than the main dig programme, with a degree of philosophical distance. I am currently working on a new version of *Time Team* that is much nearer to the original in tone, form and cost. I shall look forward to seeing if there are still archaeologists who are willing to join us and see what amazing things can be achieved in just three days!

ABOVE: *The team at Henham Hall from series twenty – still enjoying the experience!*

WHAT HAPPENS TO THE FINDS?

People often ask what happens to the finds collected after a _Time Team_ dig. Wessex Archaeology is responsible for their safekeeping from the point of recovery to their final resting place in a museum.

First of all, it's vitally important that we know where the finds have come from on each site, and we do this by labelling them with the number of the deposit (or 'context') from which they came (see mini skills masterclass on page 184)

Washing is the next step in the process and, if not completed on site, this is the first thing we do once the finds have been returned to our offices in Salisbury. Once clean, the finds are marked with the site code and context number, and put into clean bags marked with the same information. This is time-consuming, but it's essential to ensure that all the finds from each project are kept together.

Then it's over to the specialists. For each context, the finds are divided into different types (pottery, animal bone and so on) and the quantities recorded. All this information goes straight into a computer database. Experts will then look at the finds to extract information about the site. Here are some of the questions that we ask of the finds, and how the answers can help us to interpret the site.

What is it made of?

Before we can answer any other questions about the finds, we have to determine what they are made of. This is usually a simple visual process of

RIGHT: _Anglo-Saxon jewellery prepared for storage._

dividing broken fragments into ceramics (pottery, brick and tile, clay pipes), stone (worked flints, quern stones and whetstones, building stone), bone (animal and human bone, worked-bone objects), glass (vessels, windows, objects such as beads), metalwork (coins, objects made of iron, copper alloy, lead and other metals, and the debris from metalworking) and organics (wood, leather, shale and jet). Sometimes we may have to use a microscope to look more closely at an object, and some detail may only become apparent after a conservator has cleaned an object, for example a gilt coating on a copper alloy brooch, like the example from Barrow Clump (see page 87).

How old is it?

This is usually the first thing that anyone asks when an object is found. Objects can help us to date a site, so that we know when it was occupied and for how long. Some finds are better at providing this information than others – pottery and coins, for example, can often be dated quite closely by comparison with examples from elsewhere. Other objects aren't in themselves datable (animal bone, for example), but can be dated by association with other more datable finds.

Where does it come from?

Sometimes it is possible to tell where a particular object was made. For example, some pottery can be linked with a known kiln or production centre. One of the better-known examples of this is the fine red Roman tableware known as samian ware, which was made in Gaul and is very distinctive in colour, texture and finish. Many vessels were actually stamped by the individual potters, which gives us an even better clue, as there are published lists of known samian potters.

We can often identify a particular source area for stone objects such as quern stones for grinding corn, using geological identifications and sometimes even links to a specific quarry. The chalk gaming piece from Brancaster, for example (see page 45), may have come from quarries nearby to the south, or from the shores of the Wash to the west.

China from the military training camp at Belton Park (see page 197) was stamped with the marks of various manufacturers, which showed that the army was being supplied from several different sources. Information of this kind helps us to work out how connected the inhabitants of a site might have been to large-scale production and distribution networks, or whether they were largely self-sufficient.

How was it made?

Many objects will have been deliberately manufactured from raw materials – pots from clay, flint tools from natural nodules, metal objects from ore. By looking closely at the objects, we can try to reconstruct the process of manufacture. Goods may have been manufactured at household level, or production may have been more specialized, such as the very large-scale production of samian ware. By looking at objects such as the Saxon brooches from Barrow Clump (see page 87), or the decorated floor tiles found at Northwood (see page 180–1), we can appreciate the very high level of expertise demonstrated by these craftspeople.

What was it used for?

Sometimes the function of an object is obvious – for example a metal knife, or a ceramic brick – but in other cases it may be less clear. Many pots, particularly those from earlier periods, were probably not made with any specific function in mind, and could have been used for various things, such as food storage, preparation or serving. Functional information can help us to understand some of the activities that were taking place on a site, such as the presence of spindle

ABOVE: *Not all Roman pottery finds are small sherds!*

whorls and loom weights, which would indicate textile working.

What were people eating?

Information on the diet of a site's inhabitants comes from animal bone, shells (from seafood), and also from the tiny seeds and other plant remains retrieved from sieved soil samples. All these can be identified to species, and the animal bone can also sometimes be aged, so we can tell how the animals were being exploited – were they being slaughtered at a young age for meat, or kept for wool or milk, or used as working animals?

What does it all mean?

All this information is used to prepare a report on the finds. There are several criteria to be considered here. How large is the assemblage of finds? Are the finds of intrinsic interest, or do they conform to well-known and commonly occurring types? On many of the Roman villa sites that *Time Team* has excavated, large quantities of ceramic brick and tile have been recovered. After a certain point, the addition of more fragments will add no more new information – these are common finds, which generally conform to a fairly limited range of shapes and sizes.

What happens next?

It's important that finds are returned to the area in which they were found. We try to place them in the nearest local museum, unless the landowner wishes to retain them. This process can take quite a long time, as museums have limited storage space. Human bone may be excluded from this in cases where our licence to excavate human remains includes a clause specifying that the bone is to be reburied.

The crucial point here is accessibility. The finds, along with the site records, form the project archive, and this should always be accessible to future researchers, who may want to revisit a site and reinterpret the results.

Lorraine Mepham, Wessex Archaeology

INDEX

Page numbers in italic refer to illustrations

ACKNOWLEDGEMENTS

I would like to extend my thanks to the following people, without whom this publication would not have been possible: Jacqueline Stinchcombe, book coordinator; and Jo Rees Howell, lead researcher, for her committed development and editorialization of the masterclasses.

My grateful thanks also to Lorraine Mepham and Steve Thompson from Wessex Archaeology for their advice and help with the *Time Team* finds archive, and to John Allan and Tom Cadbury at the Royal Albert Memorial Museum & Art Gallery, Exeter, for their advice and guidance on pottery.

As always it been a pleasure to see the pictures of Victor Ambrus.

I would like to express my deepest gratitude to those who have contributed to the book: Naomi Sewpaul, Dr Cassie Newland, Paul Blinkhorn, Richard K. Morris, Jackie McKinley, Rob Hedge, Tracey Smith, Raksha Dave, Danni Wootton, Richard Osgood, Sergeant Diarmaid Walshe, John Gater, Ian Barclay and James Adcock.

And I would like to thank all of this year's producers, directors and production staff for their hard work on the latest series of *Time Team*.

Finally, a big thank-you to the publishing team: Doug Young, Michelle Signore and Phil Lord at Transworld, designer Nick Avery and project editor Karen Ings.

Tim Taylor

PICTURE CREDITS

TRANSWORLD PUBLISHERS
61–63 Uxbridge Road, London W5 5SA
A Random House Group Company
www.transworldbooks.co.uk

First published in Great Britain
in 2013 by Channel 4 Books
an imprint of Transworld Publishers

A CIP catalogue record for this book
is available from the British Library.

ISBN 9781905026838

Addresses for Random House Group Ltd companies outside the UK
can be found at: www.randomhouse.co.uk
The Random House Group Ltd Reg. No. 954009

The Random House Group Limited supports the Forest Stewardship Council® (FSC®), the leading
international forest-certification organisation. Our books carrying the FSC label are printed
on FSC®-certified paper. FSC is the only forest-certification scheme supported by the leading
environmental organisations, including Greenpeace. Our paper procurement policy can be found
at www.randomhouse.co.uk/environment

Designer: Nick Avery Design
Project editor: Karen Ings

Printed and bound in Great Britain by
Butler Tanner & Dennis Ltd

2 4 6 8 10 9 7 5 3 1